COMPUTER SYSTEMS TECHNIQUES

Development, Implementation
and Software Maintenance

Dedication
*This book is dedicated to the memory
of my loving parents.*

COMPUTER SYSTEMS TECHNIQUES

Development, Implementation and Software Maintenance

Jag Sodhi

TAB Professional and Reference Books

Division of TAB BOOKS Inc.
Blue Ridge Summit, PA

FIRST EDITION
FIRST PRINTING

A Petrocelli book

TPR books are published by TAB Professional and Reference Books, a division
of TAB BOOKS Inc. The TPR logo, consisting of the letters ''TPR'' within a large
''T,'' is a registered trademark of TAB BOOKS Inc.

Copyright © 1990 by **TAB BOOKS Inc.**
Printed in the United States of America

Library of Congress Cataloging-in-Publication Data

Sodhi, Jag.
     Computer systems techniques.
     Includes bibliographical references.
     1. System design.   2. Software maintenance.   I. Title.
QA76.9.S88S665   1990   004.2'1   89-20466
ISBN 0-8306-3376-6

TAB BOOKS Inc. offers software for sale. For information and a catalog, please
contact TAB Software Department, Blue Ridge Summit, PA 17294-0850.

Questions regarding the content of this book should be addressed to:

     Reader Inquiry Branch
     TAB BOOKS Inc.
     Blue Ridge Summit, PA 17294-0214

Technical Editor: Roman H. Gorski
Production: Katherine Brown
Series Design: Jaclyn B. Saunders

Contents

Preface   ix

Acknowledgments   xv

Section I: Computer Systems Origin

1 Computer Systems   3
Study of a Computer System   4
Computer System Feasibility   4
Computer System Requirements   5
Request for Proposal   5
Algorithm to Estimate Time and Cost   9
Bidder's Commitment   10
Summary   13

2 Computer Systems Project   17
Organizational Planning   18
Computer System Project Planning   19
Estimating and Scheduling   21
Project Management Techniques   24
Summary   29

Section II: Computer Systems Software Engineering Techniques

3 Techniques for Computer Systems Software Engineering   **33**

Computer Software Development Methodology (CSDM)   33
Structured Techniques for CSDM   46
Phases of a CSDM   52
Modeling a System   53
Summary   57

4 System Requirements Logical Analysis   **59**

System Context Diagram   61
System Requirements List   61
Logical Data Flow Diagram   63
Guidelines for Partitioning   67
LDFD Proposed Standards   70
Properties of a Good LDFD   71
Summary   76

5 Managing Data   **77**

Data Dictionary   77
Files Structure   80
Database Concept   81
Entity Relationship Diagram   81
Summary   83

6 Logical Specifications   **87**

Structured English   87
Decision-Assisting Devices   89
System States Transition Diagram   93
Summary   94

7 System Logical Design   **97**

Top-Level System Structured Design   98
Object-Oriented Design   101
Data Structured Design   102
Develop a System Software Test Procedure   103
Plan a System Software Acceptance Procedure   103
Products of System Logical Design   103
Summary   104

Section III: Computer Systems Software Development and Implementation Techniques

8 Program Logical Design   109

Top-Down Concept   109
Logical Flow Chart   111
Program Design Language   113
HIPO   114
NS Charts   114
Pseudo Code   114
If-Then-Else Statements   117
Nested If-Then-Else Statements   118
Establish Coding Conventions and Standards   118
Products of Program Logical Design   119
Summary   120

9 Computer Systems Implementation   121

Coding Languages   121
Unit/Module Testing   122
Component Software Component Testing   122
System Integration Testing   126
System Documentation   127
System Productivity   128
Acceptance by the Customer   128
Evaluation   129
Summary   129

Section IV: Computer Systems Life-Cycle Software Maintenance Techniques

10 Computer Systems Software Maintenance   133

Types of Computer Systems Software   133
Why Maintenance Is So Expensive   135
Techniques for Maintaining a Computer System
Software   138
Summary   145

11 Systems Life-Cycle Software Maintenance   **147**

Software Requirements Changes   147
System Software Modeling   149
System Software Analysis   149
System Software Design   150
Software Changes Summary   151
Summary   152

Appendix   Acronyms and Abbreviations   **153**

Bibliography   **155**

Index   **159**

Preface

Computer Systems Techniques: Development, Implementation and Software Maintenance is designed to provide a comprehensive picture of a computer system software, from the initiation of a system, management of a computer system project, the software engineering life cycle and development, to implementation and maintenance of a computer software in accordance with DOD-STD-2167. The prerequisite is an introduction to computer software analysis, design and programming or equivalent practical experience.

The book may be used to design software engineering or to serve as a reference for someone who is already familiar with the subject. It may be used as a textbook in a course to learn system analysis and design on one's own. It may be used as a reference to manage and maintain a system.

Computer Systems Techniques is a tutorial introduction to the computer system analysis and design. In teaching the subject, the book takes time to explain complicated matters thoroughly, with generous explanations. The exposition emphasizes the concerns of the practicing system analyst and designer, not theoretical principles. As a reference, the book contains a complete description of the details a system engineer/analyst needs when analyzing and designing a practical working system.

WHY "COMPUTER SYSTEMS TECHNIQUES"?

The book introduces various available computer systems techniques. The computer is a by-product of World War II and a necessity due to man's evolution. During its infancy in the 1950s and 1960s, computer hardware was extremely expensive, whereas an overabundance made manpower inexpensive. Despite the advancements of technology, the computer still needs the interaction of human analysts, designers, programmers and operators to make it work.

The business, scientific and medical industries quickly realized the value of computers. Management, however, concentrated on dealing with humans and was not oriented toward the problems of computer software. They were strictly interested in producing results.

To organize, implement and execute a computer system in those days often took a great toll on the computer specialists who, at the time, were mostly programmers. Overwork coupled with the stress to produce sometimes pushed them to the limit. Lack of training and communication drove many of them to look for other careers. All these factors combined to produce lengthy, undocumented programs which were unmaintainable. The result was disastrous. It became necessary to rewrite many of those systems with proper documentations to save cost.

In the 1970s, E.W. Dijkstra introduced the word *structured* into the computer industry. The idea was to make things systematic or put them in an order which is easy to understand and can be followed by others.

Many colleges and universities introduced structured techniques to computer sciences courses in the late 1970s and the 1980s. The direction of the computer industry changed completely. Computer professionals accepted the idea of structured methodology and techniques for designing and developing system software.

The Department of Defense established a standard which is referred in DOD-STD-2167. The standard contains requirements for the development of mission-critical computer system software. It established a uniform software development process that is applicable throughout the system life cycle. This standard is intended to be dynamic and responsive to the rapidly evolving software technology field. As such, it should be selectively applied and tailored to fit the unique characteristics of each software acquisition program.

This book takes care to make the reader comfortable with system concepts; for instance, how to write a Request For Proposal (RFP), how to respond to an RFP, project management, managing a system, software engineering, system analysis, system design, implementation of a system and maintenance of a system. There may be references to many other related subjects that are beyond the scope of this book and cannot be discussed in detail. Many books have been written to discuss those topics, but there was a need for a book to present a complete picture of the computer systems software: thus, *Computer Systems Techniques*. This book is the outgrowth of a continuing education course in Structured Analysis and Design that I have had the privilege to teach to degree-holding students at various universities.

APPROACH

Computer systems techniques cannot be taught simply by enumerating rules and standards. Therefore, many realistic examples and real-time system examples have been added to explain the theory. The reader will benefit from practical case studies as discussed in various chapters. Examples and exercises have been carefully crafted to be neither too simplistic nor too complicated; they have been well tested in my classes and are workable. Good systems techniques have been emphasized throughout the text. Guidelines are provided, for example, on how to draw a good data flow diagram, writing a good Request For Proposal (RFP), checklist to respond to an RFP, guidelines to tailor specific standards, and techniques to develop and maintain a system.

FLIRTATION WITH ADA*

Ada is the result of an effort by the U.S. Department of Defense to control the increasing cost of its software engineering, development and maintenance. The U.S. Air Force, Army, and Navy each began to look for its own standard language. Ada was selected after a lengthy process, and the Ada language reference manual was adopted as Military Standard 1815. A revised manual was published in July 1982 under the designations "Draft Revised Military Standard 1815A" and "Draft Proposed ANSI Standard Document for Editorial Review."

Ada Programming Support Environment, or APSE, was developed to provide support for the entire project team throughout the life of a system. The goal is to tailor the tools of design, editing, compilation for various target machines, debugging aids, test drivers, management support, configuration and program analysis aids to meet APSE requirements.

The Ada language supports many modern software engineering methodologies, such as OOD and Data structured design. Tailoring of standards like DOD-STD-2167 suitable to its own needs and related to Ada are discussed in the book.

ORGANIZATION OF THE BOOK

The book is divided into four sections: Computer Systems Origin, Computer Systems Software Engineering Techniques, Computer Systems Software Development and Implementation Techniques, and Computer Systems Life Cycle Software Maintenance Techniques. The logical flow of various sections in the book is shown in Figure A.

Section I contains two chapters and is basically meant for those who are involved in project management or computer specialists who are involved with RFPs and would like to know more about the subject.

Chapter 1 contains introductory material. It briefly provides the feasibility study to write a request for proposal (RFP). The chapter also explains how to respond to an RFP. This chapter is important for those who want to know the origin of a computer system.

Chapter 2 contains the initiation of a computer system project. It deals with establishing the project team in phases. The chapter explains the guidelines for managing a project team and project management techniques. For example, a

---

*Ada is a registered trademark of the U.S. Government, Ada Joint Program Office (AJPO).

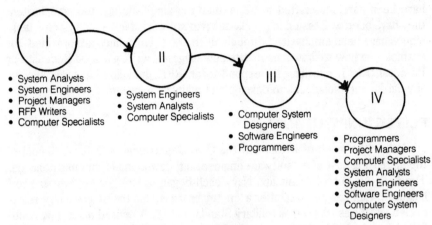

Figure A   Logical Flow of Sections and Chapters

good manager establishes a technical training program to train other members of the project team. The project manager's goal is to achieve success. Some effective management tools are also discussed in this chapter.

Section II consists of five chapters and is recommended to system engineers, system analysts or computer specialists who want to know more about software methodologies, standards, software engineering, software development and software requirements analysis.

Chapter 3 deals with the available software engineering methodologies and DOD-STD-2167. The impact of Ada language upon software engineering is discussed. The chapter includes guidelines on how to select a methodology to develop a system software. It discusses the advantages of structured techniques, and includes various phases of developing and modeling a computer system software.

Chapter 4 is possibly the most important chapter in the book. It covers the analysis of the software requirements: State-of-the-art techniques are discussed for identifying independent functions. A practical case study is introduced and the solution is explored in detail; a real-time case study is also discussed.

Chapter 5 explains the managing of data. Types of data dictionaries and classes of data are also discussed, along with entity relationship diagram.

Chapter 6 deals with documentation related to the system requirements analysis. Structured English to be included in mini specification is also discussed in addition to decision tables and decision trees.

Chapter 7 presents the preliminary design of the system. Many topics like top-level design and hierarchy are discussed. The impact of Ada language and DOD-STD-2167 on system design is also explored, and the importance of a software development file (SDF) is highlighted.

Section III, consisting of two chapters, deals with development and implementation of the system software. The independent functions identified in Section II are transformed into computer software components and decomposed into units. These units are further coded and tested. The system is finally integrated and tested to present the customer the result along with proper documentations.

Chapter 8 presents a detailed system design. Many topics like program design language (PDL), HIPO and NS charts are discussed.

Chapter 9 covers implementation of a system. Some coding guidelines, and unit testing in a generic form are discussed.

Section IV consists of two chapters and presents the maintenance of a computer system software. The section can stand on its own, despite references to topics which have been discussed in the previous chapters.

Chapter 10 covers how to maintain a computer system in general.

Chapter 11 presents techniques for maintaining software. It covers system analysis, design and necessary documentation. The chapter covers source and object code maintenance, which is the key component of the maintenance. Topics like updating SDF and software change summary are discussed.

Acknowledgments

Several students, friends and colleagues have contributed in building the material of this book to make it presentable to readers.

The comments of Terri Christensen and the publisher's technical review led to significant improvements. I am grateful to Orlando Petrocelli, who persistently encouraged me to complete the book. I initially promised him I'd send the manuscript in just a few months, after I had transformed my lectures into a textbook; instead, it took me a few years. I am grateful to the staff of the publisher who promptly responded to my calls and helped me in forming the book.

I also thank the members of my family and my wife who carried the load, and accepted it on top of their own responsibilities and duties.

Acknowledgments

Section I
Computer Systems Origin

1
Computer Systems

A computer system consists of procedures, methods and structures established to accomplish an organization's objectives in an orderly manner. It generates data and information that must be analyzed and acted upon in order for the organization to be successful. That's why it is called an *information processing system*. A system is originated at the request of the user, or by a management directive or departmental request to solve immediate problems.

The technology of the world in which we live is governed by systems of all types:

- Real-Time
- On-Line
- Knowledge-base
- Menu-driven
- Batch
- Expert

According to the dictionary, a *system* is defined as "a regulatory interacting group of items forming a unified whole." Some examples of systems are:

- Solar system
- Human body
- Highway system
- Defense system
- Government
- Bookkeeping, Payroll, Income-Tax system

Often a user says, "Can't you try to improve the existing system? What a mess!"

So, let us improve our existing system.

As noted earlier, an information processing system generates data and information, which must be analyzed and acted upon. Often, this is crucial to the success of a business.

Electronic techniques, like computers, are used to process such data to produce information that can be used to successfully run a government, and private, public and scientific industries.

In many industries, systems are studied thoroughly to establish whether they should be automated or not. When it is established that a system should be automated on a computer, a team of experts is assigned to develop and implement that computer system.

STUDY OF A COMPUTER SYSTEM

A preliminary study is conducted to delineate and assess the system. It is a fact-gathering endeavor and its objectives are to:

- Study the current system
- Identify whether a real problem or need exists
- Understand the current system and the changes to be made
- Define the problem
- Determine that the problem identified can be solved by a computer
- Compute the cost of change
- Compute risk factors of change
- Evaluate the impact of proposed changes on

    - Personnel
    - Morale
    - Training
    - Productivity
    - Technical factors
    - Economic factors

- Generate guidelines for computer system feasibility

COMPUTER SYSTEM FEASIBILITY

A feasibility study is conducted to identify alternative solutions and differentiate manual processes from automated ones depending on economic, operational and business factors. The objectives are to:

- Analyze the computer system
- Confirm plans that the system can be automated on a computer

- Analyze alternate solutions and their characteristics including

  - Methods
  - Costs
  - Benefits
  - Risks

- Evaluate and recommend alternate plans
- Generate requirements definitions

COMPUTER SYSTEM REQUIREMENTS

A requirements study clarifies the detailed functional requirements relative to the system under study. It results from the recommendations contained in the computer system's feasibility. The objectives at this phase are to:

- Reveal all potential opportunities for improvements
- Ensure that no current requirements are overlooked while defining the new requirements
- Determine functionality relative to the new requirements
- Establish performance criteria for the proposed system
- Ensure cost effectiveness
- Ensure benefits
- Confirm the reduction/elimination of risk factors
- Provide a plan for the conversion process
- Plan a future schedule
- Help prepare a Request For Proposal (RFP)

REQUEST FOR PROPOSAL

The RFP is standard in the computer industry. It is just what its name implies; a request to hardware and/or software vendors to propose in detail how they would meet certain specifications. The vendors' responses normally provide cost, timing and other necessary information that help the requestor evaluate the proposals. An RFP does not obligate the requestor to a vendor; it is merely an information-gathering activity. Proposals are usually evaluated on the basis of cost-effectiveness and other economic and practical considerations.

Definition of an RFP

An RFP outlines the need of a person, company or organization to gather information to make decisions. It can be a request to update, modify or correct an error in an existing computer system or it can be a request to design a new computer system.

An RFP may also be referred to as a work order or a specification. However, an RFP usually initiates a new project, while a work order or specification/task is typically used when modifying an existing system.

Creation of an RFP

An RFP may be generated by a user/customer or client, a department head, an information systems manager or any other responsible person(s).

Main Features of an RFP

- Ask the vendor to describe the software's ability to meet projected growth and other operational changes.
- Ask the vendor to describe the applications software: its characteristics, method of operation, special features and technical constraints.
- Ask for detailed costs, including purchase and lease prices, maintenance and other associated costs.
- Ask for an estimate of installation manpower and an implementation plan.
- Ask for a copy of the vendor's proposed contract, including responsibilities, delivery schedules, penalty clauses for missed deadlines and explicit definitions of what constitutes system acceptance.

Sample Outlines for an RFP

Section   Title

Introduction

1-0   Objective
2-0   Scope
3-0   Environment
     3-1   Function
     3-2   Problems
     3-3   Constraints
     3-4   Existing Data Processing
4-0   Current System Functions
     4-1   General Description
     4-2   Current System
5-0   New System Requirements
     5-1   General Requirements
     5-2   Proposed System
         5-2-1   Hardware
         5-2-2   Software
6-0   Project Operational Environment
     6-1   Responsibility and Resources
     6-2   Contract Personnel Resources
     6-3   Project Work Environment/Facilities

6-4   Change Control Procedures
6-5   Project Planning, Scheduling and Control
6-6   Training and Education
7-0   Project Documentation Standards and Requirements
7-1   Time Criteria and Project Milestones
7-2   Project Development Life Cycle Standards
8-0   Bidder's Responsibilities
8-1   Instructions to Bidder
8-2   Bidder's Responsibility and Contractor Liability
8-3   Payment Schedule
9-0   Deliverables
9-1   Objectives
9-2   Bid Deliverables
9-3   Project Deliverables
9-4   System Deliverables
9-5   Programs Deliverables
9-6   Final Result and Documentation Deliverables
10-0   RFP Format
10-1   General Section
10-2   Bidder's Expertise
10-3   Bidder's Clientele and Credentials
10-4   Applications/Software Proposal
10-5   Hardware/Software Network Proposal
10-6   Project Management Plan
10-7   Time Schedule
10-8   Cost Analysis
10-9   Bidder's Addendum/Exhibits
10-10 Bidder's Questions and Open Items
11-0   Proposal Evaluation Criteria
11-1   Evaluation Methodology
11-2   Evaluation Criteria

Properties of a Good RFP

Introduction. Define the purpose of the RFP, e.g. "This is an application software/hardware RFP." State whether you expect bidders to include recommendations (with cost) for hardware/software and ask them to include maintenance as part of their response.

Objectives. Define the objectives of the desired system:

- Minimizing processing time
- Man-Machine Interfaces
- The company's rules and regulations framework
- Development standards

- Specify the systems methodology
- Techniques to be followed
- Essential reports to be produced
- Maintenance of data security and integrity
- Achieving maximum system availability, reliability and file accessibility
- Reduction of operating and processing costs
- Planning for future growth
- Design of a user-oriented system

Scope. Must meet all the objectives in the design and implementation of the data processing system.

Environment.

- Define functions of user departments and their staffs
- Define problems in detail
- Define any constraints imposed by the user's policies and procedures
- Define the existing data processing hardware/software

  - Memory
  - Disk drives/tape drives
  - Printers
  - Communication network
  - Terminals
  - On line/batch system
  - Real-time system
  - Operating system
  - Programming languages
  - Monitoring systems
  - Databases
  - Artificial Intelligence devices
  - Data communications
  - Packages
  - Terminal operating system
  - Terminal progressing languages

Current Systems Function. Define in detail how the current system operates.

New System Requirements. Define the general requirements for the new system to be designed by the contractor.

Project Operating Environment. Define clearly the overall operating environment to assist the bidder in computing cost and time in his response to the RFP.

Project Documentation. It is important to specify the methodology, if any, that the bidder must follow in implementing the system, whether training and education is required and the type of documentation that is required in the RFP.

Bidder's Responsibilities. Define clearly what the bidder's responsibilities and liabilities are, including those conditions under which the contract may be canceled.

Deliverables. Define a specific time frame for project deliverables, both during the project development cycle and on conclusion of the project. The system deliverables should typically be delivered by the contractor at the completion of the contract.

Format of the RFP. It should be clear, concise and straightforward.

Proposal Evaluation. Define what factors will be considered in selecting a contractor:

- Technical expertise
- Cost
- Time
- Meeting all the requirements in the RFP
- Reputation

Response to the RFP

The bidder's response to the proposal is in accordance with the statements of work as described in the proposal and should not deviate in any way from that approach. The bidder can add state-of-the-art techniques but must keep the response within the scope and guidelines of the RFP.

Evaluation of an RFP

An RFP may consist of hundreds of pages. The best approach to preparing an RFP is to prepare a sheet for each main requirement:

- Number of outputs
- Number of calculations in a given time period
- Hardware detail
- Software detail
- Estimated manpower
- Estimated cost
- Estimated time

ALGORITHM TO ESTIMATE TIME AND COST

The vendor's goal is to make money by reducing costs and increasing profits. The goal is not only to save money and time, but also to get the best service from the vendor. Keeping these points in mind, try to:

- Minimize the risks
- Maximize use of your resources
- Plan and control effectively
- Build in decision points throughout the process
- Avoid excessive maintenance later on
- Achieve consistency

Risk is always highest at the beginning of any venture. For example, as you leave your home to go to a destination ten miles away, your risk is higher at the start because of the time you will be exposed to possible mishap, but your cost for gasoline will be at its lowest. The closer you come to your destination, the lower your risk becomes and the greater your cost of gasoline.

That situation is analogous to developing a proposal for implementation. The risk is high in the beginning and the cost is low, but risks decline and costs rise as each implementation stage is reached.

To estimate cost, consider what is really involved in the main phases of the project:

- Planning
- Study
- Design
- Implementation

What problems and risks may be encountered in each phase? You should estimate the time needed to complete each phase based on the skills and experience of the staff. Calculate personnel costs using established hourly rates and all other types of costs, such as traveling and living expenses, materials and supplies, and computer costs.

BIDDER'S COMMITMENT

The bidder should carefully review the requirements as outlined in the RFP statement of work (SOW) and select a staff that represents a blend of talents to satisfy these requirements. The overall qualifications of the staff should be demonstrated in the proposal and should include:

- Current position
- Applications experience
- Education
- Computer experience
- Citizenship
- Employment status

- Computer languages
- Operating systems
- Database management system
- Documentation standards
- Customer interface
- Structured methodology

The key to success will be the experience and technical knowledge of the data processing professionals who are performing the work.

Guidelines for Bidder's Pricing Proposal

Following is an example of a service rate cost proposal.

A. Description of Direct Services	Estimated Hours	Rate/Hr	Estimated Cost
EDP Manager	1000	$25.00	$25,000.00
EDP System Analyst	500	20.00	10,000.00
EDP System Designer	500	20.00	10,000.00
EDP Programmer	2000	15.75	31,500.00
EDP Operator	100	10.00	1,000.00
TOTALS			$77,500.00

B. Description of Overhead	Estimated Hours	Rate/Hr.	Cost

C. Administrative Expenses
60% of Schedule A

Total Estimated Cost = A + B + C

COVER LETTER

FROM:

TO:

_____ is pleased to submit the following proposal to

_____. This is submitted in response to Request For Proposal
(RFP) No._____ covering _____.

As stipulated in the RFP, the proposal has been divided into
_____ covering,

_____

_____

In submitting this proposal, we acknowledge our commitment to provide highly
qualified data processing professionals capable of meeting your requirements.

_____

_____

Sincerely,

Bidder's Checklist

(The Bidder is sometimes also referred to as the Offeror.)

1. Personnel Experience
   Contract Manager
   Reserves

2. Bidder's Qualifications

   2.1 Background
       Brief history
       Capabilities
       Organization chart
       Financial stability
       Corporate commitment
       Employee retention

   2.2 Past performance and experience
       Contract/Attribute Matrix
       Contract Briefs

   2.3 Project organization
       Brief history of Computer Systems Development (CSD)

CSD managers' qualifications
Project organization: relationship to corporate structure
Task monitoring
Predefined schedule
Progress monitoring
Reporting of expanded hours
Monthly reporting
Upper management review procedures
Corporate management resource support
Personnel
Finance
Payroll
Security

2.4 Staffing approach
Planned recruiting sources
Background checking
Selection criteria
Retention method

2.5 Compensation
Benefits
Overtime

2.6 Local labor market conditions

3. Computer System Development Plan (CSDP)

4. CSDP Whole Life Cycle Description

5. Software Engineering Development Plan (SEDP)

6. Software Maintenance Plan (SMP)

SUMMARY

Figure 1.1 shows an overview of an RFP. The goal for the vendor, in responding to the proposal, is to win the bid. This is illustrated in Figure 1.2.

The vendor submits the proposal response in a timely manner and in the best possible form in view of the RFP to win the bid. In responding to the proposal, the vendor's goals are to show how it will increase efficiency and save time and cost. To achieve these objectives, the vendor should establish the following:

- Structured plans
- Standards

- Guidelines
- Procedures
- Teams to contribute

The recommendations are graphically represented in Figure 1.3.

The vendor appoints a proposal manager who is familiar with responding to proposals. The proposal manager is responsible for organizing teams to write the response and verify that all the aspects of the RFP and statements of work in the RFP have been dealt with satisfactorily.

In Figure 1.4, TEAM A consists of technical experts, consultants and advisors who are versatile in their technical fields. Their job is to provide technical knowledge in response to the statements of work as outlined in the RFP. They will create a file called "PROPOSAL RESPONSE."

TEAM B consists of technical writers, illustrators and typists. Their job is to convert the proposal's rough draft from Team-A into formal technical writing and illustration. The typist will key in the file "PROPOSAL RESPONSE."

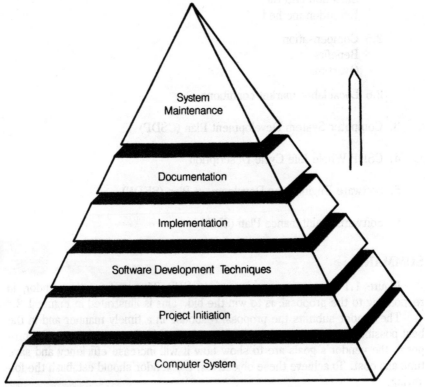

Figure 1.1. RFP overview.

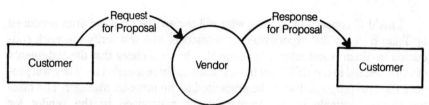

Figure 1.2. Vendor's goal.

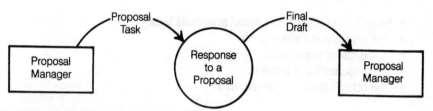

Figure 1.3. Response to a proposal.

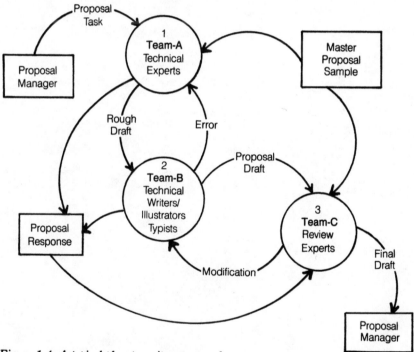

Figure 1.4. A typical plan to write a proposal.

TEAM C consists of experts who will review the proposal draft produced by Team B. They are experienced professionals who will verify the work conducted by Team A and refined by Team B. They will check that the statements of work defined in the RFP have been satisfactorily responded to. They will produce the final proposal draft to be presented to the proposal manager. The master proposal sample is the permanent file maintained by the vendor for reference and guidance. This file should contain the following:

- Sample of previously accepted proposals bids
- The organization's standards
- Introductory paragraphs
- The organization's history
- The organization's achievements

All the teams will have access to this file. The proposal response is the temporary file created by Team A, modified by Team B and utilized by Team C.

2

Computer Systems Project

Once a proposal has been accepted by the customer and the "go-ahead" is granted to initiate a project to develop a computer system software, the vendor appoints a project manager. The project manager begins to carry out the plan by setting up a team of professionals.

Requirement of a Project Manager

The project manager may appoint a system manager to carry on his duties to supervise the development of a particular computer system. The following criteria should be carefully evaluated when choosing:

- Technical Qualifications
- Communication and interpersonal skills
- Systems management experience
- Managerial skills

Responsibilities of a System Manager

The system manager is a decision maker whose main responsibility is to complete the development of the system on budget and on time. Some of his other responsibilities are:

- To develop and implement decisions relating to planning, policy making, task and goal setting, forecasting and budgeting.
- To develop a contingency plan to meet unforeseen circumstances.
- To maintain honest and open relations with project management.

- To achieve the objectives and goals of the project within the established schedule, budget and procedures.
- To redefine goals, responsibilities and schedules as necessary.
- To plan, organize, lead, motivate and delegate.
- To control the project outcome by measuring and evaluating performance against established objectives and standards.

ORGANIZATIONAL PLANNING

An *organization* is a structured use of human resources designed to meet objectives. The organizational structure defines reporting relationships, duties and responsibilities. The organization, which should be formed as soon as the project objectives have been established, should be designed to enable the resources to work effectively in units. To establish an effective organization, the system manager may choose one or more combinations of three alternatives:

1. Functional—personnel remain strictly within their assigned positions in the hierarchy. Management is ultimately responsible for decision making. Middle- and lower-level managers/ supervisors are assigned to departments, which are further divided into functional units headed by team leaders. The advantages of this structure are:

   - It is easier to manage specialists if they are grouped into one department.
   - The training and experience improves by mutual support among the group members.

   The disadvantage of this structure is the difficulty of coordinating activities among functional areas.
2. Pure Project Organization—here all personnel are assigned to a system project as one organizational unit. This structure is also called *direct organization*. The project manager is given authority for the system project and can acquire resources from inside and outside the company as needed. Personnel are assigned to only one system project until it is complete. Although the system project organization promotes teamwork and a sense of esprit de corps, it can also lead to duplication of effort, problems with "empire building," and a tendency for project management to retain personnel longer than necessary. In addition, competent personnel may move on when the system project expires.
3. Matrix Organization—this is a multidimensional structure that tries to maximize the strengths and minimize the weaknesses of the project and functional structures. It balances objectives and provides coordination across functional departments.

Experienced observers know that no one approach is perfect for all project situations. The best solution is contingent upon the key factors in the environment surrounding the system project.

COMPUTER SYSTEM PROJECT PLANNING

The beginning of the project is the time to set the tempo for the project. The project should be clearly defined by steps, and a project book, for tracking, should be started when the project is put into action. This book should be maintained throughout the project and include:

- Limitations
- Checkpoints
- Overall plan outline of the project
- Tasks
- Reports
- Changes
- Recommendations

A well-defined plan allows the project manager to anticipate unforeseen events and react before it is too late to avoid extensive damage. A plan improves current operating decisions and forecasts what the future is likely to be. Planning should be an ongoing effort during the project.

Ideally, there should be a separate plan to achieve success for each phase. After the initial phase, plans for each succeeding phase should be developed before the current phase has been completed. This will facilitate continuous funding and staffing, while minimizing slippage in the overall schedule. It also helps in measuring the project's progress. Planning activities should include:

- Project initiation
  - Budgeting
  - Scheduling
  - Goals
- Defining tasks, objectives and activities
- Staffing
- Organization
- Estimates
- Establishing methodology
- Selecting tools
- Project monitoring
- Inter-relationships among colleagues
- Definition of major tasks and activities

Budget Plan

The assigned budget must sufficiently allow for costs to effectively complete the different phases of the project. The budget should allow for expenditures such as materials, computer costs, travel and temporary living expenses.

Setting Goals

The project manager must set short-term and long-term goals to make the project cost-effective, efficient, timely and profitable. In summary, these goals are:

- Managerial effectiveness
- maximum efficiency
- increased profits
- highest quality
- better services
- effective communication
- maintenance of high morale and good attitudes
- motivation development

Setting the short-term and long-term objectives is a strategy of planning for movement in the direction that management wishes to take, while meeting the goals and needs of the participants. Setting objectives helps meet project goals in the following ways:

- It is a motivational strategy, since individual commitments and subsequent accomplishments lead to a higher degree of satisfaction.
- The greater the focus and concentration on results, the greater the likelihood of achieving them.
- Progress is measured only by work done.

Staffing

Plan to establish a team suitable to the size of the project. You don't have to create the whole team at once; you can plan in phases, depending on the number of people, skills, duration and degree of involvement required for each phase. Assign responsibilities after careful consideration of each participant's qualifications, experience and motivation. Sometimes it is necessary to arrange training if qualified participants are not available.

Delegation of Functional Responsibilities

The project manager has a list of his position's major responsibilities and also those of the subordinates reporting to him. He identifies his subordinates by brief titles and makes a list of major responsibilities:

- Manager
- Assistant Manager
- Supervisor—administration
- Supervisor—technical training/consultant
- Supervisor—analysis
- Supervisor—design
- Supervisor—programming
- Supervisor—production
- Supervisor—data base
- Supervisor—data dictionary
- Supervisor—quality
- Supervisor—audit
- Supervisor—configuration management
- Task Leader—analysis
- Task Leader—design
- Task Leader—programming
- Team Leader—programming
- Team Leader—operations
- Coordinator
- Librarian
- Task Leader—documentation

Defining these responsibilities and duties helps a manager build the organization. He can prepare a long- and short-term organization by filling first the positions relating to the most immediate demands and filling the others later as they are needed.

ESTIMATING AND SCHEDULING

A project manager should keep a record of tasks and activities plotted by sequence in time against actual completion versus planned completion. One of the methods of achieving this is the Earned Value Technique.

$$\text{EARNED VALUE} = \frac{\text{Actual to Date (ATD)}}{\text{Estimate at Completion (EAC)}}$$

The earned value represents the percentage of completion of a project in terms of effort accomplished as a portion of the total effort required. It is customary not to identify an earned value in excess of 85 percent until the project is completed (100 percent). This avoids the "99 percent complete syndrome." For a large project, it is often beneficial to portray cumulative Earned Value.

PERT Technique

Program Evaluation and Review Technique (PERT) was initially designed to help identify and relate the many steps involved in complex projects. The technique has been used to deal with a wide range of nonrepetitive planning and control problems. PERT is a special application of network analysis for estimating and controlling the time required for activities and work packages about which little information from past experience is available. PERT network analysis consists of:

- Specifying tasks to be completed
- Sequencing and inter-relating work packages
- Setting up the network
- Scheduling

Events are connected by activities. Because events are end items (results or products), they take no time, money or resources themselves. Activities, however, require all of these things.

The following are suggested guidelines for drawing a PERT network:

- It should be developed by a person familiar with and committed to the project's objectives and requirements.
- The development should start with the ultimate targeted objective and proceed backward to the beginning event.
- During development, there are often questions about each end item. The activities that must be completed before this event is reached should be outlined.
- An activity cannot begin until the event or end item preceding it has been completed.
- Wherever possible, two or more end items and their associated activities which can be accomplished concurrently should be set up in parallel paths.
- A *critical path* should be identified to discover the longest cumulative time needed to accomplish end items and their associated activities. (The entire project will be held up if they are delayed).
- A slack path should be identified to discover the shortest cumulative time needed to accomplish end items and their associated activities.

A sample is shown in Figure 2.1.

To estimate time for PERT activities, three time estimates are obtained from all the activities of the network:

$$\text{TIME EXPECTED (TE)} = \frac{T_o + 4\,T_m + T_p}{6}$$

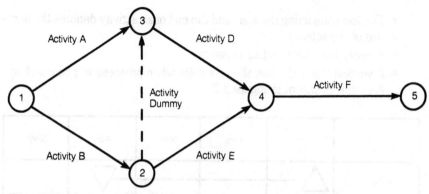

Figure 2.1. A typical PERT network showing activities that must be performed and their sequence.

Where:

TE = Expected Time, which considers the effects of both favorable and unfavorable conditions.

T_o = Optimistic Time, which is an estimate of the minimum time an activity will take if unusually favorable conditions are experienced.

T_m = Most likely time, which is an estimate of the normal time an activity would take if it were repeated an indefinite number of times under identical conditions.

T_p = Pessimistic time, which is an estimate of the maximum time an activity will take if unusually unfavorable conditions are experienced.

Gantt Technique

The Gantt chart planning technique, created around 1900 by Henry L. Gantt, is often used for scheduling. It shows activities, their duration and the relationships among them. Commonly, it is known as a bar chart.

The advantages of a Gantt chart are:

- It forces management to plan carefully.
- It can be produced easily using pencil, paper and ruler.
- Management can compare at a glance work planned versus work accomplished.
- It can be understood easily.
- It gives a large amount of information on a single piece of paper.

Symbols used in a Gantt Chart are:

- The start of an activity.
- The end of an activity.

- The line connecting the start and the end of an activity denotes the duration of the activity.
- A heavy line shows actual progress.
- A vertical "dotted" line shows a point when progress will be checked. A sample is shown in Figure 2.2.

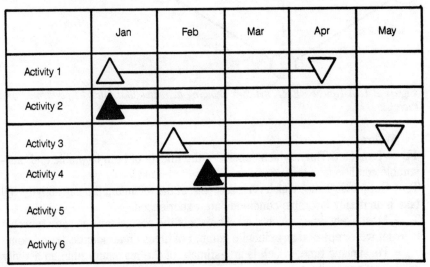

	Jan	Feb	Mar	Apr	May
Activity 1					
Activity 2					
Activity 3					
Activity 4					
Activity 5					
Activity 6					

Figure 2.2. Gantt Chart showing a project planned versus actual activity.

PROJECT MANAGEMENT TECHNIQUES

Project management is a state of mind. The project manager must accept that a project can attain specified results on time and within budget, despite complexity and change. Accepting these factors will ensure that the direction of the project itself will be controlled by managerial techniques that will remain operative within these constraints. Good management discipline can lead to good project management.

Functions of Good Project Management

A good project manager must be familiar with the following functions.

1. Planning
   - Forecast
   - Objectives
   - Policies
   - Strategy
   - Goals
   - Budget

2. Organization

   - Purpose
   - Resources
   - tasks

3. Staffing

   - Requirements
   - Recruitment
   - Training
   - Compensation
   - Promotion
   - Termination

4. Control

   - Objectives
   - Standards
   - Measurements
   - Reporting
   - Correction

5. Direction

   - Leadership
   - Authority
   - Motivation
   - Communication
   - Coordination

Develop Milestones

Developing a graphic representation of work effort by time is accomplished by developing a milestone chart as shown in Figure 2.3.

Ideally, a milestone should represent the analysis of the work effort, tasks and activities plotted by sequence in time with the provision of tracking actual completion versus estimated completion.

Establish Control

Control consists of comparing progress achieved against the desired plans. Appropriate corrective actions should be taken in case the result has deviated from the plans.

The control should be established from the start of the project and continue until it is completed. This can be achieved by developing a milestone which is firm, specific, defined, measurable and scheduled by tasks.

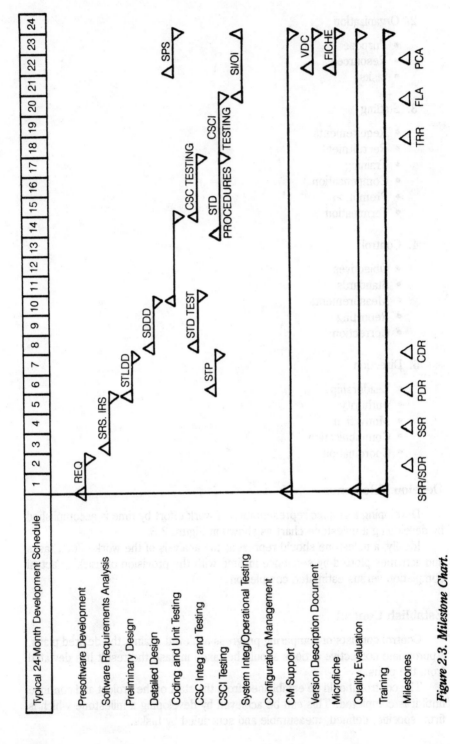

Figure 2.3. Milestone Chart.

Monitor the project resources, such as budget and personnel, on a regular basis. Modify immediately any variance from the plan. Determine the status of the project progress through formalized reporting techniques; this will build the path of communication. This path is accessible to all concerned people so that the project is completed on time and within budget and specification.

Establish Standards

A project manager should establish standards to be followed by all members of the project. These standards should be related to work. Sometimes there is no alternative except to accept standards like DOD-STD-2167 and Ada which are recommended in the RFP. These can be tailored to the system requirements as mentioned in the Bidder's response and accepted by the customer.

Establish a Technical Training Program

The project manager should establish a task-oriented technical training program for the members of the project team. The program should fulfill the objectives and mission of the project successfully and should include, for instance, basic training of new hirees and advanced training of people already onboard to enable them to cope with new technology. This is a purposeful, people-oriented training aimed at improving job interest and job satisfaction. For the members of the project, training increases their skills which gives them a better chance for advancement, helps them to better understand what is expected, leads to less uncertainty and error in their work, and makes their job easier and safer. A training program accelerates the completion of qualitative, cost-effective products and improves work performance.

Practice Effective Communication

A project manager is continually involved in communication with his or her people. It is, therefore, necessary that the manager understands the basics of thought transfer and idea exchange. There is a need for good communication which should include exchange of ideas from the members of the team to the project manager and vice versa. A good project manager should keep an "open mind and open door" style of management. With this atmosphere, any employee can walk in and discuss matters with the manager without any formalities. A manager should have time to listen to his or her team members and show due respect for their ideas and thoughts.

Create a Workable Atmosphere

The most important role of a project manager is to create workable atmosphere for the members of the project. Team concept and walk-throughs should be encouraged. Another responsibility of a project manager is to see that members do not form cliques or groups for protection that victimize others who do not join them. The project manager should devote equal attention to all members of the project.

Interviews should not be assigned to one individual. Instead, form a small group, much like a selection committee. The selection of a new employee should depend on recommendations from all the members of that committee. Once employees are hired, they should be properly treated and trained well for their assignments. Performance evaluation should be monitored after three months, six months and on a annual basis. Inspire confidence in the new employees that they should feel at home in the organization and that they will be able to progress. It is a loss to the company when trained employees leave after a year of confirmation, time and money spent to train them.

The project manager has to be an expert at identifying an employee-related problem and at solving them. To keep employees happy at work is a great art. To motivate them to work hard, contribute and return more than one hundred percent is the greatest art. Ideally, project managers are like parents. They have to act differently at times, sometimes as a leader, a guide, a partner, a teacher and a colleague. They are responsible if their team members either become victims or leave the organization for other reasons than personal ones.

The project manager should periodically evaluate their team members' performance. Employees expect a raise and a promotion for work well done. Such recognition motivates workers to work harder. Acknowledge employee achievements.

Manpower Integration

A project manager should understand that the software design will be used by computer operators and maintained by other computer professionals. Also, the software will be integrated with hardware. There should be complete coordination among the software development team, the user's representatives and the project management in order to ensure that the system design can be operated and maintained efficiently and safely within the available manpower structure, personnel skills and training resources.

Manpower integration (MANPRINT) requires the diverse talents of experts in human factors engineering, training, safety, manpower and system software design. The human engineering activities should aim at ensuring that the software designed can be operated and maintained within the capabilities and skill levels of the expected users.

To achieve these goals, the project manager may appoint another manager to lead a MANPRINT team who will establish tasks and milestones for planning, coordinating, and integrating the MANPRINT elements and team. That manager is responsible for ensuring that the software development team is following the MANPRINT considerations.

SUMMARY

The vendor appoints a project manager to carry out the plan of computer software development who opens the communication link with the customer to accept the task for the software development to be performed. The project manager may appoint a system manager to set up a team of professionals to accomplish the task. This process is illustrated in Figure 2.4.

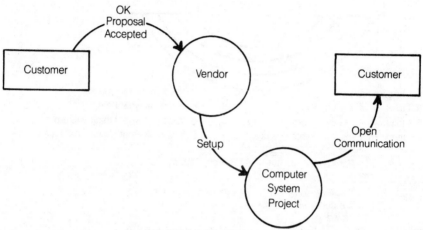

Figure 2.4. Origin of a computer system project.

Efficiency in project management can be achieved only if all staff members take a businesslike attitude toward their own work and measure their own performance of responsibilities against established goals and standards. They should all try to achieve success by constantly looking for more cost-effective techniques of developing software.

Effective communication is very important among the members of the project team and the project manager. It has been said that when two people communicate, there are eight different thought channels flowing between them. The process is formulized as two to the power three as shown in Figure 2.5.

It is important for an employee to have job security, respect, a fair and understanding boss, opportunity for advancement, colleagues, interesting work, a salary and benefits.

MANPRINT refers to the comprehensive management and technical effort to ensure total system effectiveness by continually integrating into the material development and acquisition all relevant information concerning human factors engineering, manpower, personnel, training, system safety and health hazards.

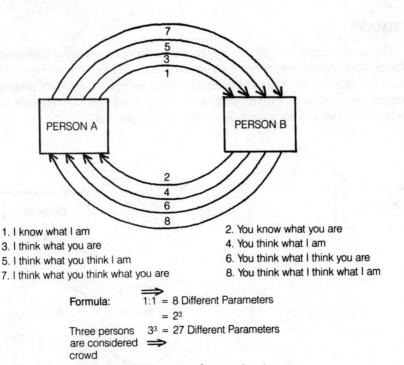

1. I know what I am
3. I think what you are
5. I think what you think I am
7. I think what you think what you are

2. You know what you are
4. You think what I am
6. You think what I think you are
8. You think what I think what I am

Formula: $\overrightarrow{1:1}$ = 8 Different Parameters
$= 2^3$

Three persons 3^3 = 27 Different Parameters
are considered $\Longrightarrow$
crowd

Figure 2.5. Communication parameters between two persons.

Section II
Computer Systems Software Engineering Techniques

3

Techniques for Computer Systems Software Engineering

Software Engineering is a disciplined and integrated approach to software development. The objective is to produce software which has certain desired properties. Four properties which are accepted as the goals of software engineering are modifiability, efficiency, reliability and understandability.

Software will be modifiable because change cannot be avoided. Changes are also required to remove errors from the software and improve the system's performance. Modifications should honor the original system design structure so that the original structure model does not become obscure after repeated changes, which in turn would make future changes more difficult.

Efficiency will be improved by recognizing and understanding problems in the early part of the software development.

Reliability will be established by formal validation. System development results in a code that is most probably correct, and a confidence exists that the system meets the required specifications. Reliability should be designed in from the start, and not added at the end.

Understandability is essential if the systems are to be modifiable, efficient and reliable. Modules should use consistent notation. The software will then be reusable, because it will be constructed in modules that adhere to established standards.

COMPUTER SOFTWARE DEVELOPMENT METHODOLOGY (CSDM)

A *methodology* (an established body of procedures) is a must in the development stages to reduce costs and save time. A clearly defined computer software development (CSDM) methodology helps not only in controlling cost in software development, but also software maintenance.

The following is a detailed explanation of standards, guides and techniques reflecting the fundamental philosophy of a methodology approach to systems management, problem solving and system development and maintenance.

Each system development is divided into phases. Each phase is described by a set of limited objectives, has a time scale short enough to be accurately planned and has a measurable end point. Each phase is further subdivided into tasks, and each task is divided into activities.

A methodology should provide suggestions for performing the individual activities in a system development. Depending on the size of the system, phases can be followed in a sequence or can be merged to meet particular requirements. A phase may consist of a number of tasks; a task may consist of a number of activities; an activity is a function to be performed

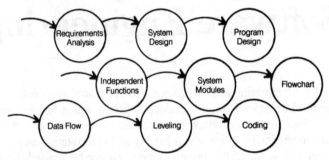

Figure 3.1. A methodology sample.

DOD-STD-2167

There are many methodologies used in system development. One example is DOD-STD-2167, an illustration of which is shown in Figure 3.2. This standard was approved in 1985 by Department of Defense for use by all departments and agencies of the Department of Defense. The standard contains requirements for the development of mission-critical computer system software. The use of this standard increases compatibility and reliability of computer systems that are critical to our nations defense. It establishes a uniform software development process which is applicable throughout the system life cycle. The software development process defines development activities which result in:

- The generation of different types and levels of software and documentation
- The application of development tools, approaches and methods
- Project planning and control

It incorporates practices which have been demonstrated to be cost-effective from a life cycle perspective, based on information gathered by the Department of Defense (DOD) and the computer industry.

Software development is usually an iterative process, in which an iteration of the software development cycle occurs one or more times during each of the system life cycle phases as shown in Figure 3.2.

Figure 3.3 describes a typical system life cycle, the activities that take place during each iteration of software development, and the documentation which typically exists at the beginning of an iteration in any given system life cycle phase.

The system life cycle consists of four phases:

- Concept exploration
- Demonstration and validation
- Full-scale development
- Production and deployment

The software requirements development cycle consists of six phases:

- Software requirements analysis
- Preliminary design
- Detailed design
- Coding and unit testing
- Computer software component (CSC) integration and testing
- Computer software configuration item (CSCI) testing

The total software development cycle (or a subset) may be performed within each of the system life cycle phases. Successive iterations of software development usually build upon the products of previous iterations as shown in Figure 3.4.

Software will be developed in accordance with this standard to the extent specified in the Vendor/Bidder's clauses, statement of work (SOW), and the Contract Data Requirements List (CDRL), unless it is permitted to tailor this standard as required.

In 1987, the Department of Defense issued the latest version of DOD-STD-*2167A*, a new standard for system life cycle software development and maintenance. A sample is shown in Figures 3.5 and 3.6.

Another standard of the Department of Defense, DOD-STD-*2168* contains requirements for the establishment and implementation of a software quality program. This program includes planning for and conducting assessments of the quality of software, associated documentation and related activities, and planning for and conducting the follow-up activities necessary to assure timely and effective resolution of problems. This standard, together with other DOD, military and company specifications, and standards governing software development, configuration management, specification practices, project reviews and audits and organization management tools, provide a means for achieving, determining and maintaining quality in software and associated documentation.

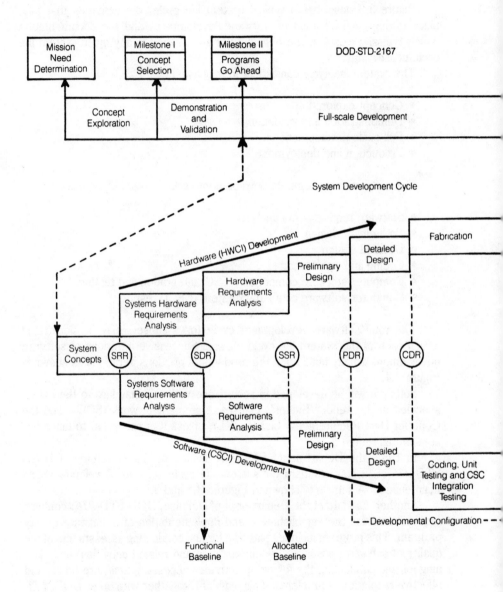

Figure 3.2. System development cycle within the system life cycle.

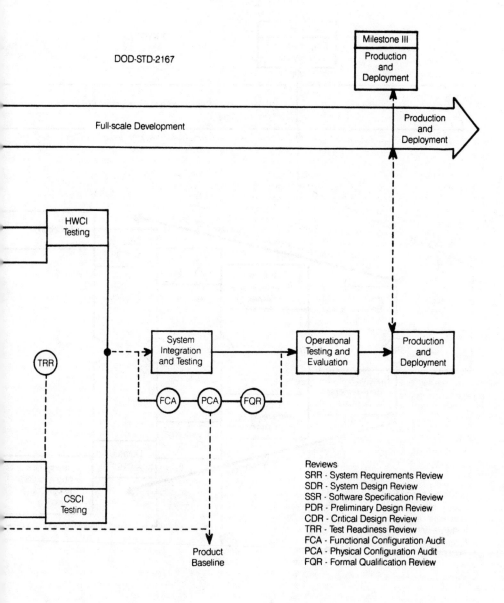

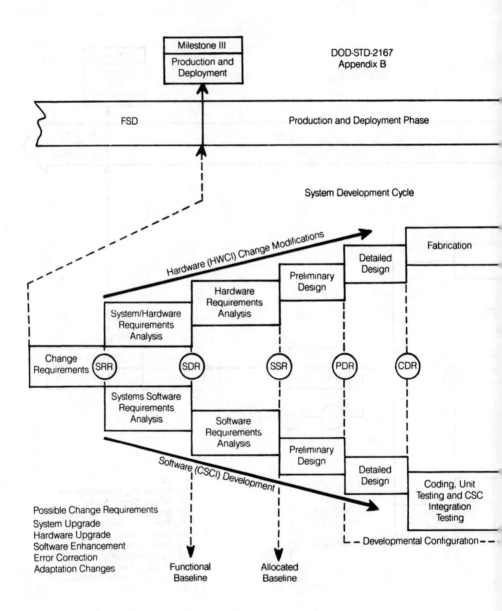

Figure 3.3. System support cycle within the system life cycle.

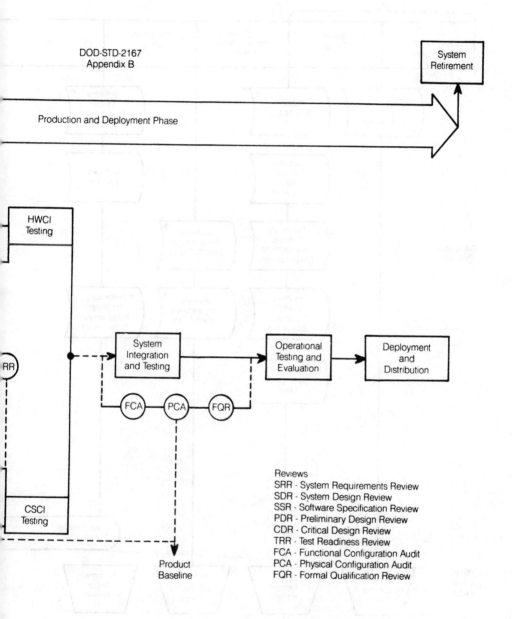

DOD-STD-2167
Appendix B

System
Retirement

Production and Deployment Phase

HWCI
Testing

RR

System
Integration
and Testing

Operational
Testing and
Evaluation

Deployment
and
Distribution

FCA   PCA   FQR

CSCI
Testing

Product
Baseline

Reviews
SRR - System Requirements Review
SDR - System Design Review
SSR - Software Specification Review
PDR - Preliminary Design Review
CDR - Critical Design Review
TRR - Test Readiness Review
FCA - Functional Configuration Audit
PCA - Physical Configuration Audit
FQR - Formal Qualification Review

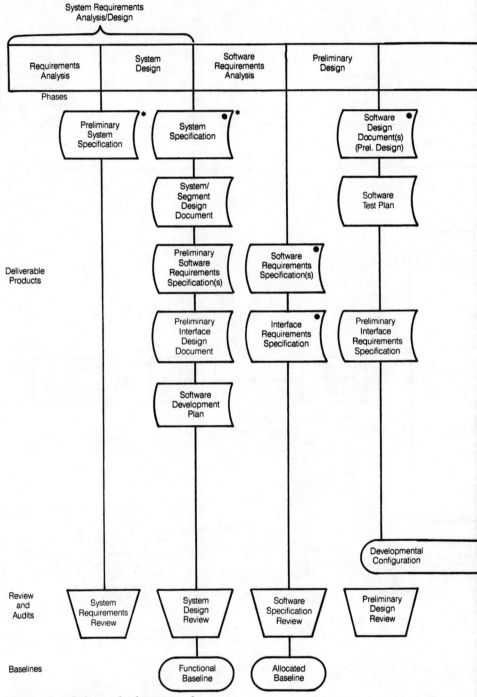

Figure 3.4. Software development cycle.

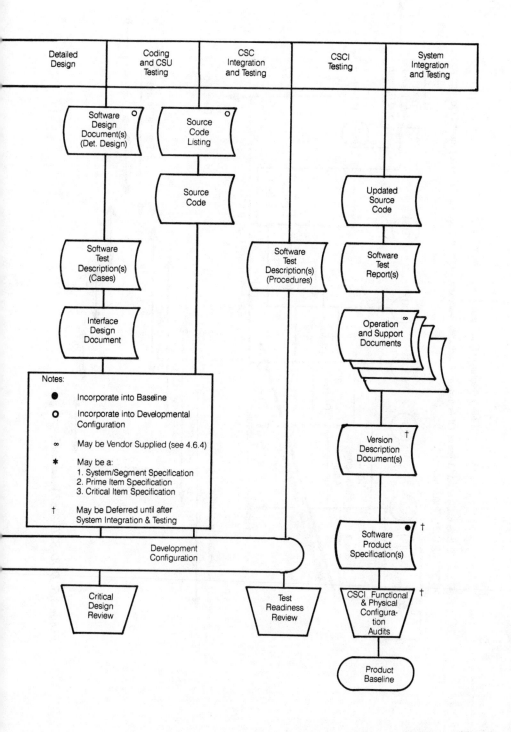

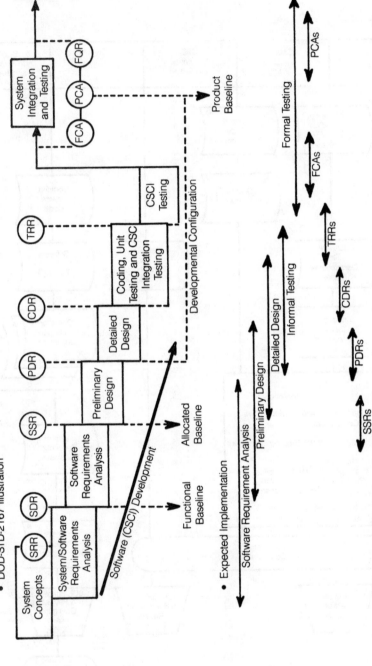

Figure 3.5. *DOD-STD-2167A standard.*

The Ada Impact

Ada is designed to meet the software engineering goals. Ada encourages the software engineering principles of abstraction, information hiding, modularity, localization, uniformity, completeness and confirmability. The standards in DOD-STD-2167A are designed to increase the readability, reliability and portability of Ada programs. That is, a program unit written in Ada can be ported from one computer to another without the need for modification.

The Ada language has no dialects, MIL-STD-1815A is another standard of the Department of Defense and is a registered trademark of the Department. Ada is a high order language (HOL) which supports concurrency with Ada tasks. Embedded applications normally refer to machine-dependent features, whereas Ada provides a means of expressing low-level machine features in a high-level fashion with representation specifications.

Ada is far more than a programming language; it is a system from which a new software culture is evolving. Predictions are that Ada will be the most important programming language of the 1990s. Programmers must have strong background in software engineering to appreciate Ada's complexity. With it, productivity gains may be achieved by using fewer lines of code, more efficient coding and the re-use of code.

It is important to start training computer professionals in Ada now. A commonly accepted training frame is six months or more to achieve proficiency. Ada cannot be taught in a conventional way. It will be taught in a software engineering context. Seminars are the best approach to teach the initial concepts. Lectures, case studies and hands-on experience should be used later, and students should be given as much practical experience as possible. Computer-aided and programmed instruction should eventually be introduced.

The computer industry must understand that Ada will stay with us despite opposition to it and that the maximum benefits of Ada will be achieved by using proper software engineering practices and training for those who will be putting it into practice.

Selection of a CSDM

The most suitable CSDM for meeting the particular requirements of a project should be selected. The goal is to deliver high-quality systems that meet the customer's needs on time and within budget. Specifically, the CSDM:

- Provides a stable, well-documented production environment
- Installs and uses proper tools for systems development
- Improves communication and relationships between customer and all system participants
- Improves analysis, design, programming and testing techniques
- Provides the user with a steady, predictable flow of information
- Improves system structuring, planning, estimating, controlling and review.

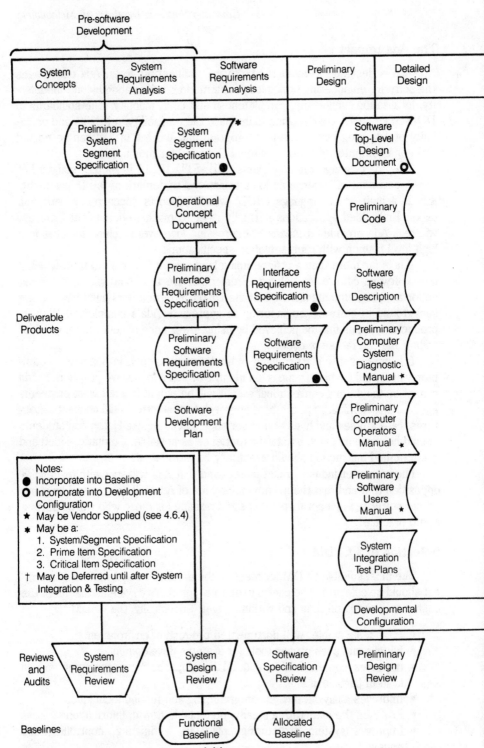

Figure 3.6. Software development activities.

44

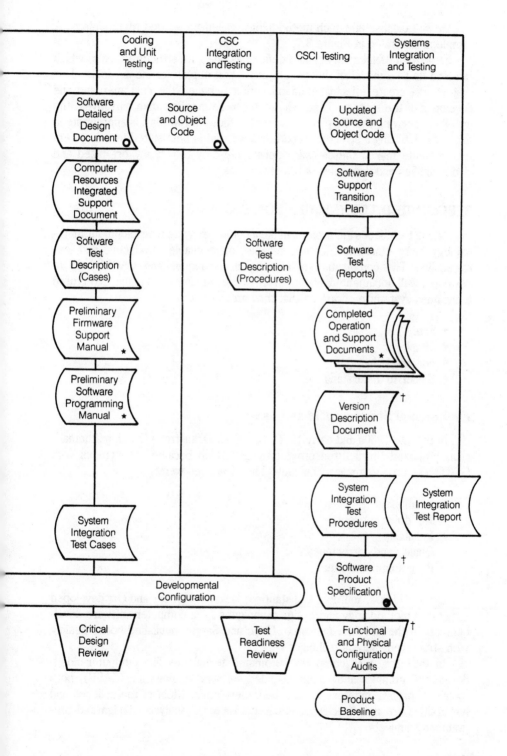

Coding and Unit Testing	CSC Integration and Testing	CSCI Testing	Systems Integration and Testing

Software Detailed Design Document ○

Source and Object Code ○

Updated Source and Object Code

Computer Resources Integrated Support Document

Software Support Transition Plan

Software Test Description (Cases)

Software Test Description (Procedures)

Software Test (Reports)

Preliminary Firmware Support Manual ★

Completed Operation and Support Documents ★

Preliminary Software Programming Manual ★

Version Description Document †

System Integration Test Procedures

System Integration Test Report

System Integration Test Cases

Software Product Specification ● †

Developmental Configuration

Critical Design Review

Test Readiness Review

Functional and Physical Configuration Audits †

Product Baseline

We will discuss one such methodology, called Structured Methodology. A sample is illustrated in Figure 3.7.

Structured Methodology can be defined as one with structured tools, which can lead us to a model of the system consisting of state-of-the-art tools. This system will create effective communication between the customer and the developer of the system. There should be more graphics than narratives, the well-known saying that "a picture is worth a thousand words" is appropriate in this case. Utilizing a structured methodology that is best suited to the system requirements makes the software development systematically organized and also simplifies and decreases development risk.

STRUCTURED TECHNIQUES FOR CSDM

These techniques are tools to make a computer system development methodology more efficient, effective, reliable, maintainable, productive and less expensive. The combination of structured techniques and CSDM help to develop a well documented system in less time. In simple language, structured techniques systemize efforts so that they are:

- Safe
- Simple
- Followable by others
- Easier to understand

Evolution of Structured Techniques

In the late 1960s and early 1970s Mr. E.W. Dijkastra, a Dutch mathematician, proposed "structured programming" which became synonymous with GOTO-less programming techniques. The objectives were:

- Readibility
- Top-down concept
- Reliability
- Quality and correctness
- Programming efficiency

In the mid-70s, Yourdon, Constantine, Jackson, Warnier and Orr developed structured methodology and design techniques for a computer software development. In the late 70s, Demarco, Gane and Sarson published books dealing with structured analysis techniques.

In the 80's, new computer automated techniques like computer-aided-design and graphics and computer-aided software engineering (CASE), both tools for analysis and design, have been developed. Most of the colleges and universities are now teaching computer structured analysis, design and programming subjects.

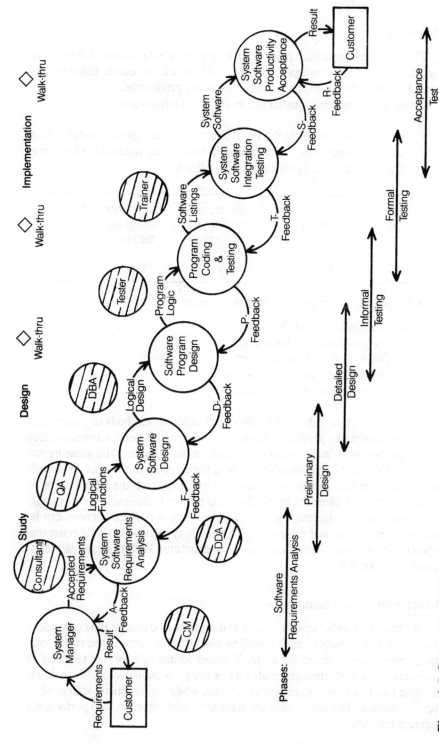

Figure 3.7. Structured methodology.

Advantages

The structured approach helps reduce or eliminate the pitfalls of developing a system, even those developed with a CSDM, which, in return, helps reduce costs. The systems are maintainable, reliable and productive.

There are several reasons for achieving these advantages:

- Enough time is spent in the initial analysis and design of a system. This makes the foundation strong enough to hold up the system for a long time without collapsing. Guidelines are as follows:

structured analysis	structured design	structured coding + unit test	implementation, integration and testing
20%	25%	40%	15%

- Eliminates communication barrier between

  - The customer and the contractor
  - The customer and the analyst
  - The analyst and the designer
  - The designer and programmers
  - Programmers and the operators

One-on-one communication implies eight different methods of conveying a message between two people, as discussed earlier in this book. Communication may be defined as an interchange of information that produces the same mental picture in the mind of the receiver as is in the mind of the sender. It is well-known that barriers to communication do exist, despite the best efforts by involved parties to eliminate them. By using proper techniques—graphics, figures, diagrams and documentations—in developing a system, barriers can be reduced, if not eliminated completely. The best way to avoid blocking communication during system development may be a Structured Walk-through, as is illustrated in Figure 3.8.

Structured Walk-Through

A structured walk-through is used to determine and ensure the correctness and quality of documentation. It should be conducted at every phase of the computer system development life cycle. Whether formal or informal, technical or non-technical, a walk-through creates a friendly professional atmosphere different than that of a meeting, review or critique, while it promotes learning, sharing, and helping. The documents are error free, cost effective, and perform the required functions.

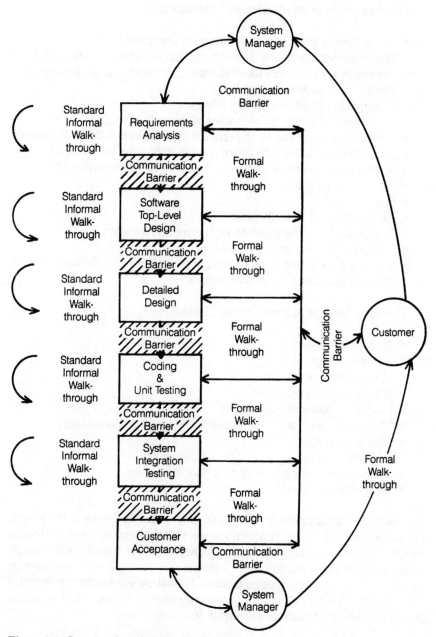

Figure 3.8. Structured walk-through scheme.

The main points of an effective walk-through are:

- The originator initiates a walk-through when ready
- The originator fills up the walk-through form as shown in Figure 3.9
- The originator circulates the walk-through form among the participants
- Two or three people participate
- Participants should have vested interests
- The originator states the objectives of the walk-through
- The originator distributes all pertinent material before the walk-through
- Lists of errors and questions are created during the walk-through
- No attempts to correct errors are made during the walk-through
- Two-hour time limit
- Show results
- No counting and "sandbagging"
- The originator takes action on each error and question
- The originator lets participants know the action taken
- The originator is free to discuss the questions raised in the walk-through with the questioner for detail if needed

The many benefits of a walk-through include:

- Early error detection
- Training is improved
- Morale will improve
- Team concept is encouraged
- Output productivity will improve
- "Ego-less team" and "team leader" concepts are encouraged
- Risk is reduced
- Easier to manage
- Increased visibility into system development
- Better project control

The walk-through participants should have vested interests in the project and should have read the pertinent materials before attending the walk-through in order to provide technical comments. Management can attend a walk-through if they meet the above requirements. Informal walk-throughs are more common and can be scheduled any time as needed. Formal walk-throughs are recorded and scheduled in advance, and are conducted either to accept, reject or accept with modifications software development documentation.

Walk-Through Form

Project (Name/Number) and Specific Walk-Through Product: _____

Initiator: _____

Description of Walk-Through Materials To Be Reviewed: _____

Date: _____ Time: _____ Location: _____

Duties	Participants	Phone #	Can Attend?	Received Materials?	Materials OK?

_____ Pre-Walk-Through Review Showed Major Gaps. Walk-Through Rescheduled For

Date: _____ Time: _____ Location: _____

Walk-Through Agenda

_____ All Participants Know and Agree To Follow Same Set of Guidelines.

_____ [ ] New Product. Walk-Through of Product.

_____ [ ] Old Product. Item-By-Item Checkoff of Previous Action Item List.

_____ Create New Action List.

_____ Reach Group Decision.

_____ Provide Copy Of This Form To Appropriate Personnel.

_____ Approved [ ] No Revisions Necessary; [ ] Minor Revision(s) Necessary
(No Additional Walk-Throughs Scheduled.)

_____ Incomplete [ ] Major Revisions Required; [ ] Review Incomplete
(Next Walk-Through Scheduled For: _____

Issues: _____

Signatures: _____

Figure 3.9. A sample walk-through form.

PHASES OF A CSDM

The main phases in a software development are:

- study/analysis
  - software logical requirements analysis
- design
  - logical system design
  - logical program design
- implementation
  - program coding and testing
  - system integration testing
  - system productivity

The overview illustrations of the software development phases are shown in Figure 3.7. These represent the life cycle of a system as follows:

1. The customer's requirements are accepted by the system/project manager.
2. The customer accepts the final output of the system to satisfy the requirements.
3. The system manager, depending on his management style and the organization structure, manages all phases and delegates responsibilities and duties to assigned personnel.
4. The system logical requirements analysis phase is the starting point for logical understanding and analyzing the requirements. In this phase we translate the requirements into the functional software requirements analysis. Structured methodology tools will help in developing a model of the system that will explain both the definition and analysis of the requirements.
5. The database department provides assistance in defining and accessing data dictionary elements for database files.
6. The logical system design phase converts the logical functional analysis into a logical system top-level modular design which will reflect the requirements defined in Phase 1. The requirements are then more completely broken down and allocated to the proper functionally associated component. This will be broken down further and allocated to functional units performing the required processing. Finally, the requirement is allocated to the module in the unit that performs the required action to produce the desired result.
7. The logical program design performs the detailed flow charting of each module to the point where it can be coded.

8. The programming coding converts the detailed design into a language coding. The code is compiled, executed and validated as software. Internal unit testing and integration testing is conducted by the programmer and properly documented to ensure that requirements have been met to achieve the desired results.

9. Integration testing of software is conducted to verify usefulness, viability, and requirements compliance of all system software.

10. All updated and approved documents and program software are submitted to the customer for authentication and approval.

11. Quality Assurance checks the quality of work and applies the techniques used in monitoring the software development process to ensure that the customer requirements are satisfied.

12. Configuration Management checks the formats of documents and maintains an audit trail of the development.

13. The system is put into actual use, accompanied by documentation such as user manuals, procedures and texts, to produce actual data.

14. The computer operation facilities runs the job in production on schedule and distributes outputs to the appropriate people.

As noted before, the ultimate goal of system development in a profit-making organization is to reduce cost and increase efficiency. A CSDM can contribute to the achievement of these goals because:

- it minimizes risks by encouraging systematic development and progressive definition of detailed requirements.
- it allows frequent reviews or decision checkpoints before starting each phase.
- it uses resources efficiently because parallel system development tasks can be carried out concurrently.
- it makes planning and control easier.
- it avoids excessive maintenance as all the documentation is developed as the system evolves.
- it shortens decision time.
- it improves communication.

MODELING A SYSTEM

Modeling a system means to introduce structured tools into a methodology. These will facilitate a system to be partitioned as shown in Figure 3.10.

A model is nothing more than an (explicitly) ordered and structured approach (procedures) for making the determination of *what, where, when and how*. Thus, in a model, you can inspect almost all the available relevant state-of-the-art tools which can not only develop a new system but also provide all the documentation necessary to maintain a system.

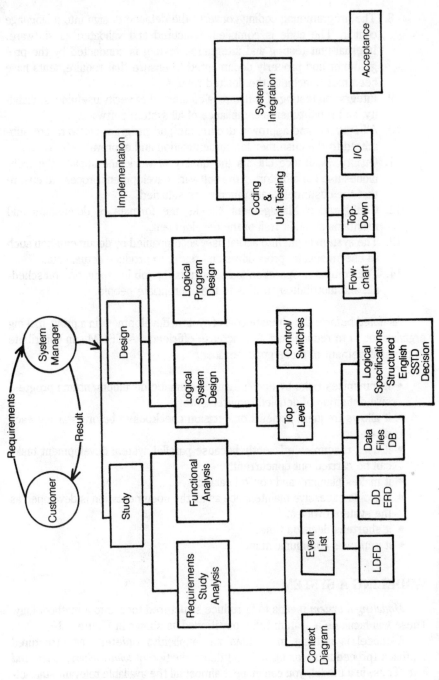

Figure 3.10. Suggested phases duration.

So, the goal of a model is to save time and cost and make the system more efficient.

It will also help:

- To eliminate the communication barrier at various stages
- To educate professionals about the system and state of the art
- To explain a system

Hence, a model:

- Has top-down break-down of a system into a model
- Offers a complete and precise description
- Is followed by functional specification

These functional specifications are used for:

- Design
- Coding

A model of a system can be developed that explains both the definitions and analysis of the requirements stated in the system specifications. A model provides complete documentation for a system plus all the necessary logical figures and tables. This method also provides flexibility in case any change occurs affecting enhancement for the future and facilitates the maintenance of the system efficiently and cost effectively.

The following tools can be used in drawing a model of a system:

- Graphics
- Top-down partitions
- Highlighting of critical features

Why do we need a model? Because it will describe the following:

- Logical link between modules/units
- Relationship between files and modules/units
- How many modules are accessing a file
- Which module will update a file
- Which module will initialize a file
- Which module will create a file
- Recording of data layouts
- Filing of layouts
- Compilation of the data dictionary at early stage
- Input/output definition

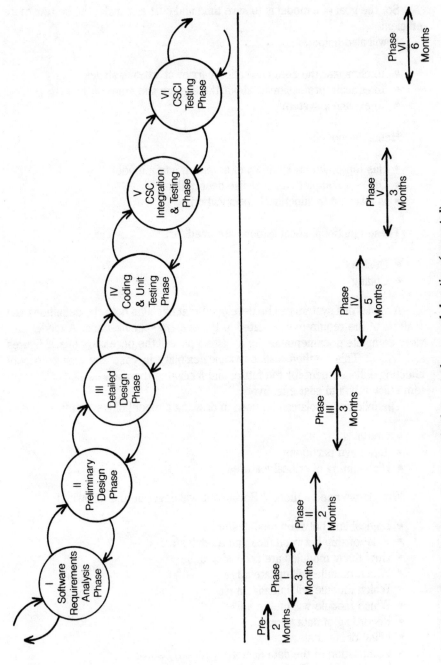

Figure 3.11. An example of software development phases and duration (suggested).

Most of this information is not available in conventional program flow charts.

Models are the starting point of good documentation. They can be a great help later on in maintaining the system and helping to:

- Understand the purpose of the system
- Understand the environment in which the system operates
- Understand the system by stating:
  - Context diagram
  - Event identification
  - Data flow diagrams
  - Data dictionary
  - Data files
  - Brief description
  - Decision-making devices
  - State transition diagram (switches/flags actions)
  - Environment relationship diagram (relationship of various files/records data)

SUMMARY

Software engineering is a disciplined and integrated approach to software development that includes four basic properties, namely modifiability, efficiency, reliability and understandability.

DOD-STD-2167, DOD-STD-2167A, and DOD-STD-2168 are methods of development developed by the Department of Defense to ensure proper standards are followed by the software developers for Defense contracts.

A clearly defined methodology helps control costs in software development. A sample development is shown in Figure 3.11 to illustrate the suggested duration of each phase in a software development.

4

System Requirements
Logical Analysis

System requirements logical analysis can be defined as the execution of the customer's requirements completely, accurately and reliably. It is the foremost phase of modeling a system. Why do we need structured analysis? A simple answer is so that we can understand the customer's requirements and communications.

System logical requirements analysis means to:

- Identify independent functions
- Help in planning, estimating and scheduling
- Identify files
- Establish logical relationships between functions and files
- Establish data dictionary
- File layouts
- Provide mini specs

The job of a system analyst is to *think* and apply personal experience to the interpretation of the customer's requirements. The requirements may not explain every aspect of analyzing the system, so the experience of a good analyst plays a bigger role in understanding, interpreting and analyzing them. Above all, it is an important duty to satisfy the customer who has originated the requirements. The analyst can use either the primitive tools of lengthy narrative for analyzing the requirements, or the state-of-the-art tools as follows.

SYSTEM CONTEXT DIAGRAM

The first step toward a good and efficient model is drawing a system context diagram. This can also be called *Main Process Diagram* (MPD). MPD comprises the topmost level of the model by defining inputs/outputs and control in real-time.

The MPD diagram can be defined as:

- The domain of study
- All inputs/outputs (high level)
- Highest-level process

The context is modeled graphically using an MPD. It describes:

- The net flows between a system and its environment, which can be
  - Data
  - Control
  - Material flows
- The people, devices and other systems in the environment which send and receive the flows

But the MPD does not describe:

- The internal details
- The entire system as packaged as one bubble (a circular representation)

Drawing a context diagram is an art. Since you are going to study the requirements of the system, you have to define the domain of study. The following parameters will help in drawing a context diagram:

- Start with a circle, presuming your system—name it
- Draw in all data inputs—arrow flows-in on the left side
- Draw all data outputs—arrow flows-out on the right side
- Give name to all data flows. This is the beginning of the data dictionary
- Show all controls and responses as dotted lines
- Show all this information from the requirements
- Make sure that the LDFD is correct for the level of detail being shown
- Don't get hung up on simple error flows
- Do not show files inside other processing
- Be prepared to start over

A sample MPD is shown in Figure 4.1.

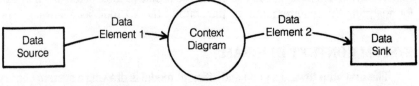

Figure 4.1. A sample MPD.

SYSTEM REQUIREMENTS LIST

It is helpful to identify the main logical functions of the system in what can be called an event list or requirements list.

The system requirements list, or event list, is a tool used to compile and define the major functional activities of the system requirements. It will further help in drawing a logical data flow diagram.

The following factors should be considered in identifying major events in the system:

- Response
- Source
- Destination
- Schedule
- Events

Thus, it is clear that an event list is extracted from the system requirements.

Response to an event occurs in the system when there is a change in state, transforming data or, both.

An event can occur which is not signaled by a flow, several flows can be associated with a single event and two or more events can be associated with a single flow.

Some hints for identifying events are:

- Requests to read data
- Requests to stop
- Processes
- Updates
- Write commands
- Delete commands

This is wrong to say in identifying events:

- Submits reading/writing requests
- Any reaction which occurs within the system

The event list will help us to further partition the main process into independent subfunctions. An event can consist of one or more requirements, a requirement can consist of one or more tasks, and a task can consist of one or more functions.

Example

The primary mission of a radar system is to detect, locate, and record an object. This information has to be relayed to an officer for necessary action.

The radar operator initializes temporary files at the start of the operation, and thus sets up the radar for function. The radar operator signals the generation of the radar beam to detect and locate the object only if the system is functionally operable. Please draw context diagram and compile an event list.

Solution is shown in Figure 4.2.

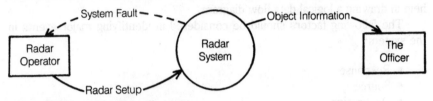

Figure 4.2. Sample context diagram.

The radar system context diagram is drawn as shown above. The function of the radar operator is shown as the data source. The data flow "radar-setup" is shown as the input to the radar system. The response "system-fault" is shown coming from the radar system to the radar operator for action. The output from the radar system is going to the officer for necessary action. As has been discussed before, this is a high-level overview of the radar system.

The radar system event list can be compiled as follows:

- The radar operator initializes radar files
- The radar operator receives radar system fault
- The radar operator generates radar beam

  - Detects an object
  - Locates the object

- The Officer receives the object information

Exercise

There is a need to establish communications between the ABC manufacturing and distributing corporation and the sales office which is about 50 miles away. This will help employees fill up orders with what is readily available in the home office storage. The corporation has ten other sales offices located at various distances. For an effective communication network, they need a transmitter and receiver at each location.

One of the duties of a communication operator (CO) is to establish a data communication link with the home office (HO).

The CO has to observe the following rules:

- transmission request must be OK'd to transmit by the receiver operator at the HO

- the message must be acknowledged by the receiver
- the transmitted message can be put on hold by the receiver operator if the receiver is busy
- the receiver operator may request for retransmittal of the message if not received correctly.

Please draw context diagram and compile an Event List.

NOTE: Assume they are using some sort of computer called DCS (Data Communication System). You may draw context diagram for one location only which can be applicable to other locations also.

The solution is shown in Figure 4.3.

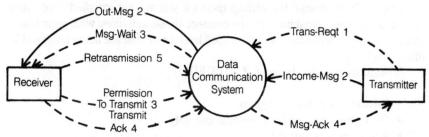

Figure 4.3. Exercise context diagram.

The sample context diagram is drawn as shown above. The data flows are numbered to help in compiling the event list.

The system sample event list is compiled as follows:

1. Transmitter (Tx) sends the transmission message request
2. Tx sends the message
3. Receiver (Rx) receives the transmitted message
4. Rx is busy
5. Rx acknowledges the message received correctly
6. Rx did not receive the message correctly

LOGICAL DATA FLOW DIAGRAM

A logical data flow diagram (LDFD) generates a top-level functional analysis of the requirements by drawing data flow diagrams for each main function and allocating requirements to the proper function. So, we can define the functional LDFD as a network representation of a system's functional components which shows the flow of data through the system. We know that drawing a LDFD improves understanding of the logic involved in the system. It also provides visibility into the design of the system.

To summarize an LDFD:

- It is a network representative of a system
- It represents the component pieces of the system and the interfaces among them
- It provides easy and graphic means of modeling the flow of data through a system

Hints for Drawing an LDFD

There is an art to drawing an LDFD. You must plan the arrangement of various functions of the system, then draw circles to represent these activities. You must be ready to change the arrangements if you are not satisfied, since they are an aid to clear thinking. Try to connect these activities with your plans; identify files to store data that can be used later on or that are being accessed by other functions.

To summarize, the drawing of an LDFD:

- Partitions a context diagram
- Delineates each activity, section and duty
- Responds to event list
- Starts at the outside
- Includes all net inputs and outputs
- Describes the composition of each data flow, and gives it a name
- Works like a jigsaw puzzle
- Reviews the data
- Uses connectivity—certain inputs are connected to outputs. A bubble is drawn in between them and is named
- Shows controls/responses in dotted lines

Example

A sample LDFD is shown in Figure 4.4.

- TM1 stands for DATA SOURCE.
- FL1 stands for DATA FLOW from TM1 to TR1.
- FL2 stands for DATA FLOW from TR1 to TR2.
- FL3 stands for DATA FLOW from TR2 to TM2.
- FL5 stands for DATA FLOW from ST1 to TR2.
- FL6 stands for DATA FLOW from TR3 to ST1.
- TR1, TR2 and TR3 stands for processes transforming the input data into the output data.
- ST1 stands for DATA file.
- TM2 stands for DATA DESTINATION or DATA SINK.

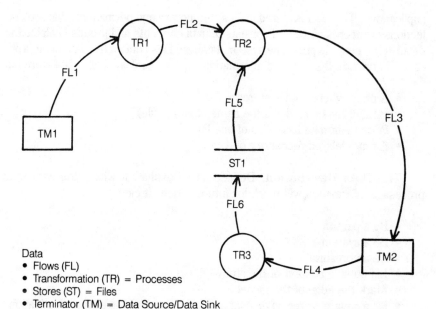

Data
- Flows (FL)
- Transformation (TR) = Processes
- Stores (ST) = Files
- Terminator (TM) = Data Source/Data Sink

Figure 4.4. A sample LDFD.

Elements of an LDFD

The Data Source. Source of data to be processed by the computer. It can be:

- A person
- A system
- An organization
- A data storage file

A square or rectangle containing the name of the source of data it represents.

The Data Flow. Defined as flow of data—inputs and outputs:

- A pipeline through which packets of known composition flow
- A named vector/arrow

The Data Process. Defined as the situation where logical instructions will be given to the computer to process the data flows—inputs and outputs. This can be further explained as:

- The transformation changes incoming flows into outgoing flows
- A circle or bubble containing a name and, usually, a number

The Data Store. Commonly called a file. A file is a repository of inter-related facts and figures stored without redundancy and available to multiple applications. This data is stored in files, temporary and permanent, that are collections of records. A record consists of data elements and groups explained in detail in the next chapter. The system database files contain the data to be processed to provide the required information. So, we can say that a data store is:

- A place where data is stored
- Parallel lines containing the name of store (file)
- Permanent data base files of one line
- A time-delayed repository of data

The Data Destination. Defined as a destination where the computer processed information will reach for future action. It can:

- Be a person
- Be a system
- Be an organization
- Lie outside context of the study
- Mark the edge of the model
- Be a square or rectangle containing the name of the source destination
- Also be called a data sink

Figure 4.5 illustrates an example of a data flow diagram.

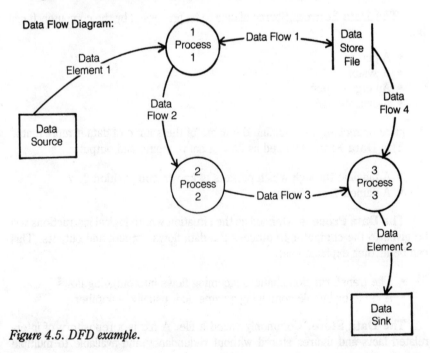

Figure 4.5. DFD example.

GUIDELINES FOR PARTITIONING

Partitioning of the LDFD is used to identify independent functions. Some guidelines for partitioning are to:

- Partition to minimize interfaces
- Concentrate on data and make sure all data flows are nameable
- Use the data dictionary to keep track of new data flows
- Refine by topological repartitioning
- Be prepared to start over

When do we stop partitioning? A functional primitive is a bubble which cannot be further partitioned and has single input and single output.

Balancing of Logical Partitioning

Balancing is very important when partitioning logical data flow diagrams. The following points are valuable in logical partitioning:

- Input and output are balanced between parent and child
- Input to the bubble (on the parent) is the same as input to the child figure
- Output from the child figure is the same as output from its associated bubble on the parent

Numbering Techniques

Logical partitioning processes should be numbered in a consistent manner, as shown in the example in Figure 4.6.

Naming Convention of a LDFD

The names of processes, files and data flows should be meaningful and related to the system. The names should be concise, not abbreviated. Examples of some names which have become conventional are *data dictionary* and *mini specifications*. These names will be carried on by others when developing system software.

Figure 4.6 illustrates an example of an LDFD.

Guidelines for Leveling

Leveling represents various partitioning sets of LDFD. The lowest level of the LDFD set cannot be further partitioned. Level 1 is the high level partition shown in Figure 4.7. Level 2 is the partitioning of each transformation process of the level 1 LDFD, until the lowest level cannot be further partitioned or is in the standard to be partitioned after a certain number of levels. Each lower level

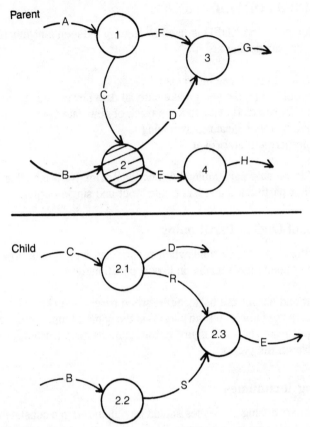

Figure 4.6. Example of a leveled LDFD.

LDFD (child) will balance with its corresponding upper level LDFD (parent).

- A single transformation may be partitioned into a group of transformations and states separating lower levels from higher levels
- An alternate representation of a network too large for conventional drafting limitations
- Allows top-down analysis, top-down specification
- Allows you to select which details to show at the top and which to show lower down
- There are no off-page connectors

In Figure 4.7, the system context diagram is shown with three data sources and data sinks. There are three inputs going into the system and four outputs coming out of the system. In the Level 1 LDFD, let us presume that the system context diagram is partitioned into four independent processes, as shown. The

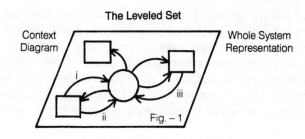

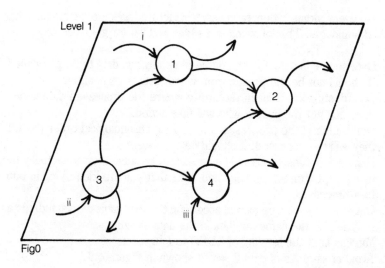

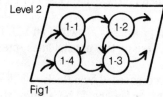

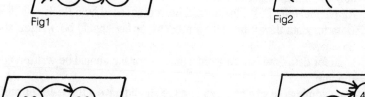

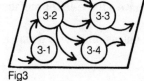

Figure 4.7. Various levels of a LDFD.

Level 1 and the context diagram are balanced. If we liked, we could show a file or two in between, but let us keep it simple here. And remember—there is always connectivity between the partitioned processes.

Let's partition the first process as shown in Level 2, Figure 1. The LDFD is balanced, and the partitioned processes are hypothetically placed and connected. Similarly, we can partition the other processes as shown. We can continue to level as long as the processes cannot be further partitioned.

LDFD PROPOSED STANDARDS

Almost every organization professing structured system techniques has established standards. The following is a suggested list for guidance only:

1. Data source is actually the source of generation data to be processed. It should not be the person from whom data is originating.
2. Data destination is again the entity where the processed data is destined and not the people who will take action.
3. Numbering of the processes should be in chronological order the way they will be processed; it should be consistent.
4. Names of processes should be consistent because they are actually the name of programs, modules and units that you are identifying in bubbles/processes.
5. Data Flows should be named according to the organization standards as they will be the names of data in the data dictionary.
6. You can limit the leveling of LDFD to four levels.
7. Avoid criss-cross of data flows as shown in Figure 4.9.
8. You can limit the length of name of data flows.
9. Some of the data flows can be explained on the same page of LDFD if space permits.
10. Ideally, there should be five or seven processes shown in an LDFD.
11. All temporary files should be represented by two parallel lines, preferably in a horizontal position.
12. All permanent (DB) files should be represented by a thick solid line.
13. Data for data flow input into a process or file should be written above the line.
14. Data for data flow output from a process or file should be written below the line.
15. Data coming out of a process or a file should have a three-letter preface related to the process or file.
16. Response should be considered of one BIT unless otherwise defined.

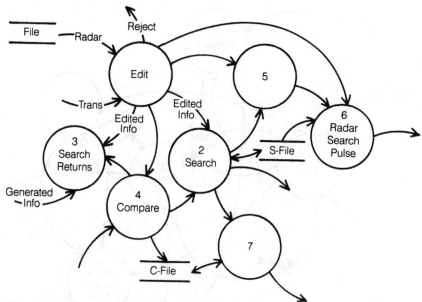

Figure 4.8. A sample LDFD (recommended).

PROPERTIES OF A GOOD LDFD

A good logical data flow diagram should possess the following properties:

- Neat and clean
- Easy to follow
- Easy to understand
- Properly labeled
- Well documented
- Sequentially numbered
- Logical representation of the requirements

It should be drawn according to the standards established by the organization. A sample LDFD is shown in Figure 4.8. Another example of the same LDFD, but poorly executed, is shown in Figure 4.9. Such an LDFD is not recommended.

Some of the common errors committed by students are shown in Figures 4.10 and 4.11. In Figure 4.10, the conditional data flows should not be shown as IF-NOT-OK and IF-OK; data flow *synchronize process* is not correct; the data flow *credit-trans* is not properly destined; and the data flow from the source

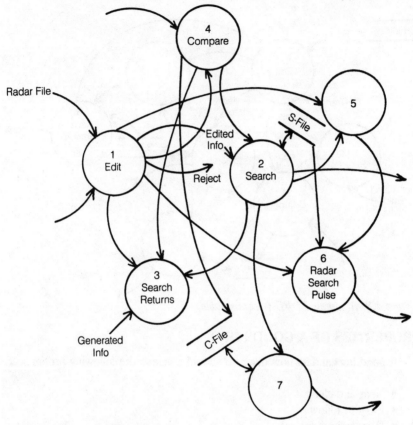

Figure 4.9. A sample LDFD (not recommended).

credit voucher is not marked. In Figure 4.11 process #2 is not receiving any data to be processed. Process #3 is receiving all the data but has nothing coming out of it. Finally, the names are not meaningful.

Case Study: Balancing Your Checkbook

You are proud to have a checking account at "The Universe Bank." You are free to write as many checks as you want, as long as you have enough money to cover them in the account. The bank has a good reputation, and there is a $10.00 charge for every check that bounces; they don't want to keep customers whose checks bounce regularly.

Common Errors

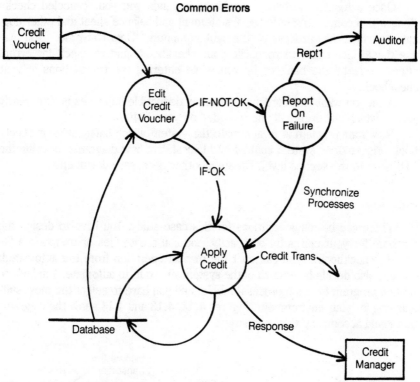

Figure 4.10. Look for errors.

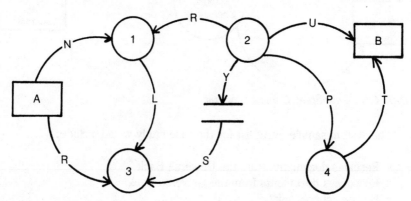

Figure 4.11. Find errors.

Once a month the bank's bookkeeper sends you your canceled checks along with a computerized financial statement and balance sheet and other documents which they process on the bank computer "Data Universe." You may use these documents to reconcile your checkbook, and to check for errors either made by the bank or by you while entering the transactions in your checkbook.

Also, you want to record any annual tax deductible expenses in your yearly journal which will eventually be recorded on your 1040 tax form.

Now your problem is to automate the system which balances your checkbook. Please draw system context and logical data flow diagrams, drawing the LDFD up to the second level. Create all other necessary documents.

Solution

There can be many solutions for this case study. You have to design the software for your computer's capacity. You can create files or merge in a file called "checkbook." You can split the manual operation from the automated; you can also decide how much of the system you want to automate. You have to write a program for each process/bubble, and you have to select the most suitable one for your environment. Figures 4.12, 4.13 and 4.14 show the diagrams that could accompany this case study.

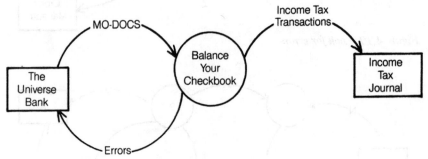

Figure 4.12. Case Study Context Diagram.

The system sample event list for the case study would include:

- Receives documents from the Universe Bank
- Reconciles documents from the Universe Bank
- Updates checkbook
- Resolves errors/discrepancy
- Updates income-tax journal

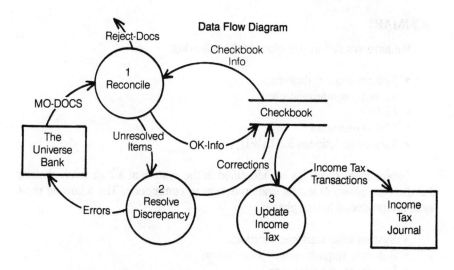

DD: MO-DOCS = [Cancelled Checks + Deposits + - - - - -]

Figure 4.13. First-level LDFD.

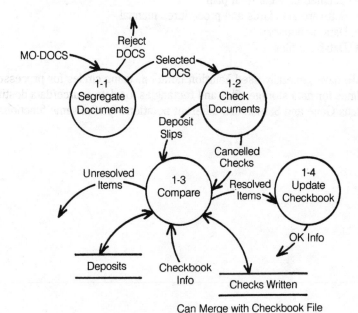

Can Merge with Checkbook File

Figure 4.14. Second-level LDFD.

SUMMARY

We have studied in this chapter the following:

- System context diagram
- System requirements list
- LDFD
- LDFD elements
- Various techniques for LDFD

Independent functions are identified in the system at a high level, allowing for the next phase of logical system design to commence. The following products are produced in this phase:

- System functional specifications
- Software requirements specifications
- Interfaces specifications
- Updated software development plans
- Updated quality assurance plan
- Updated configuration plan
- Software standards and procedures manual
- Data dictionary
- Database files

We have generally used Yourdon notation, using circles for processes, parallel lines for data storage, files and rectangles for data source/data destination, whereas Gane and Sarson use different notations for the same functions.

5

Managing Data

A computer handles data only. So far, we have discussed the flow of data—where it is coming from and where it is going—while identifying independent functions that will process that data. Now we are going to define that data.

Data consists of numeric, alphanumeric or alphabetic contents. Data needs to be input in a proper format to be processed properly. A computer will process that data into intelligent information.

For example, data can be a date, say, 03021987. This information is not very useful to many people if they don't know that it is a date. A computer can process the data and convert it into intelligent information, such as 03/02/1987, or 03-02-1987 or 2 Mar 1987.

DATA DICTIONARY

Compilation of data in chronological order is defined as a *data dictionary*. This is a tool for managing data resources. The data dictionary is a set of definitions for data items in groups and elements as declared in the LDFDs for all data flows and data stores. The compilation of data is converted into intelligent information. Thus, we can define a data dictionary as a repository of data about data.

The purpose of a data dictionary is to record and coordinate data so that any changes, additions and deletions of data may be uniformly conducted, and it will consist of global definitions of data groups and elements that are acceptable to others who are involved in the software development and maintenance.

Advantages

- Improved productivity
- Improved quality
- Global data definition
- Uniformity of updating data
- Centralized updating of data
- Customer satisfaction
- Improved communication
- Memory conservation
- Maintenance of standards
- Easy access by database files

Definition of Data Dictionary Elements

The elements of a data dictionary can be defined as:

- The meaning of the item
- The domain of the element by specifying limits
- Whether the element is discrete or continuous:

    − Discrete = item-type
    − Continuous = customer-name/price

Requirements

The requirements of a data dictionary are that it be:

- Accessible by item name
- Nonredundant
- Concise
- Logical
- Limited (definitions only)
- Correlated to LDFD

Classes of Data

There are basically two classes of data:

- Group: shows the component data that make up the group and the relationships among them
- Element: the lowest level data that cannot be divided into smaller pieces; they may or may not be components of a group

Data Group. A name of a person can be considered a data group. For instance, Jag M. Sodhi consists of:

- First name (data element)—Jag
- Middle name (data element)—M.
- Last name (data element)—Sodhi

Let us study another example. Let's say the date is 20 Mar 1987. The date is a data group, whereas the data elements are:

- Day—20th
- Month—Mar
- Year—1987

We can say that a data group is composed of at least one or more data elements. A data element is a single logical item of data. In addition, we can use mathematical symbols to represent data composition.

CUSTOMER-NAME = {FIRST-NAME + (MID-NAME) + LAST-NAME}

Here, "=" stands for "consists of" or "composed of"; "{ }" stands for "iteration of"; "+" stands for "and"; and "( )" stands for "optional."
    Let us take another example.

PAYMENT-MODE = [CASH I CHECK I CREDIT-CARD]

**The selection of data element names is important as these will be carried on by others developing the system software.

Here, "[ ]" stands for "choose only one of"; "I" stands for "or"; and "**" represents any "comments."
    Data Element. A sample of completed data element definition form: (Refer to the case study in Chapter 4).

System Title:	BALANCING CHECKBOOK
Entry Name:	MONTHLY DOCUMENTS FROM THE "UNIVERSAL BANK"
Mnemonic Name:	MO-DOCS
Composition:	[{CANCELED-CHECKS} + (DEPOSITS) + (OVER-DRAFT) + INTEREST-EARNED + (DEDUCTIONS) + MISCELLANEOUS]
Alias:	- - -

Data type:	ALPHANUMERIC
Field Size:	- - -
Author:	JOE SMITH
Modified Date:	09/23/86
Created Date:	03/29/83

Exercise

Define data dictionary for the following:

1. The monthly bank statements package consists of canceled checks, deposits, advertisements, any overdraft, any interest and tax information.
2. You are going to attend a "Structured Analysis" seminar in New York City. You have reserved your ticket and must pick it up at the airport counter. You go to the airport to catch the flight. Once the ticket agent gets the completed ticket, she asks for payment. She says, "We accept payments only by cash, check or credit card. Also, I need to see proper ID if the payment is other than cash."
3. Please correct the following:

   TOTAL-ITEM-PRICE = SALE-PRICE + SALES-TAX

Suggested solutions:

1. BANK-PACKAGE = [{CANCELED-CHECKS} + {DEPOSITS}
                    + {(ADVERTISEMENTS)} + {(OVERDRAFT)}
                    + {(INTEREST)} + TAX-INFO]
2. ACCEPTED-PAYMENT = [CASH I CHECK I CREDIT-CARD+(PROPER-ID)]
3. TOTAL-ITEM-PRICE = SALE-PRICE + (SALES-TAX)

FILE STRUCTURE

Data dictionary assists in the organization, control and utilization of data by providing a central, updated source of information about data. It also assists in accessing various data files and in manipulating data to generate the desired intelligent information.

The data is stored in files that are collections of records. A record consists of data elements and groups. Thus,

- Files are iterations of records
- Most files have a field that is used as a key for access

Files are sometimes created out of necessity. These have to be approved by the data base administrator. Similarly, creation of or changes in the composition of a data element or group has to be approved by the data dictionary administrator. There are two types of files—*temporary* and *permanent*.

Temporary Files

Temporary files are created for the following reasons:

- To keep data temporarily, then to have it erased after its usefulness is past
- To keep data temporarily, but initialize the data in the files periodically.

For example, temporary files are useful to create when:

- You don't want to keep data for long
- You set up the system in different environments and must reinitialize to put new data parameters each time.

Normally, these files are represented by two parallel lines.

Permanent Files

As the name suggests, these files are permanent and the data within the file is permanently retained, and they can be updated but not frequently erased. Permanent files, also called database files, are normally represented by a single solid line.

DATABASE CONCEPT

A database file is a repository of interrelated facts and figures stored without redundancy and available to multiple applications. This data is stored in *files,* which are collections of records. A *record* consists of data elements and groups. The system database files contain the data the user wants to process into information. A telephone book is the perfect example of a file. Each page is a record, and the customer information on each page is the data. There are many types of databases on the market and many books are available to explain them in detail. However, explaining the topic in detail is beyond the scope of this book.

Figure 5.1 shows the relationship among a data dictionary, files and data flows.

ENTITY RELATIONSHIP DIAGRAM

An Entity Relationship Diagram (ERD) depicts the stored data within a system as a network of objects connected by dependent relationships. This is a high-level overview diagram of data which is in strategic top-down planning. Top-down planning of data identifies the entity types involved in the system and determines the relationships among them. Use of ERDs will improve the system design and functionality by providing an accurate representation of the many relationships among the system data elements.

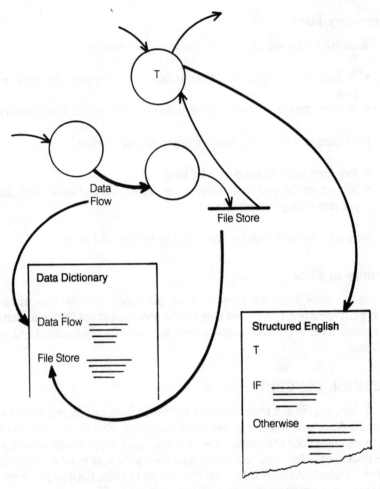

Figure 5.1. Relationship between data dictionary files and data flows.

Objects are representations of things which can be properly named and uniquely identified. They can be also a set of data elements. Relationships are named associations between two or more objects. These are represented as:

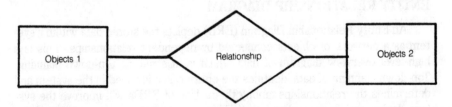

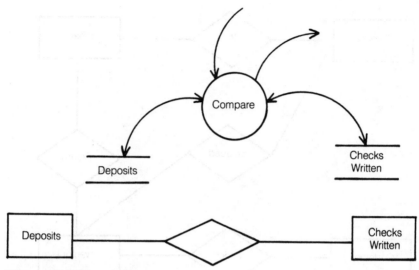

Figure 5.2. ERD sample.

Guideline for drawing on ERD:

- Compile event list
- Draw LDFD
- Project the data transformation of files
- Identify relationship of objects

An example of an ERD is shown in Figure 5.2.

There are two other techniques for entity relationship data modeling. Both represent the relationship between individual records. These techniques are:

- Chen Entity Relationship Data Model
- Merise Entity Relationship Data Model

In a Chen diagram, the relationship is represented by a diamond. An icon drawn between data records is itself an entity and is labeled with descriptive information about the relationship as shown in Figure 5.3.

In a Merise diagram, the relationship entity is represented by an oval. The rectangular icons representing objects are also different, since they are labeled with descriptive information about the relationship as illustrated in the Figure 5.4.

SUMMARY

Some of the tools for data management are discussed in this chapter—data dictionary, data elements and data groups. Data elements are the smallest unit

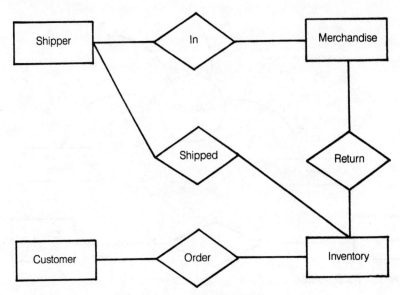

Figure 5.3. Chen Entity Relationship Data model.

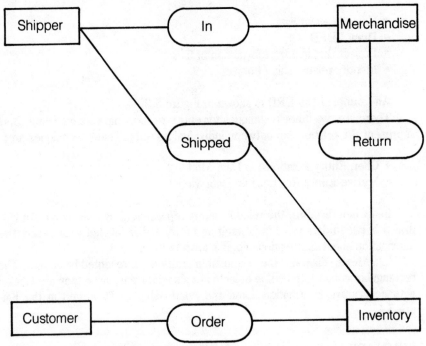

Figure 5.4. Merise Entity Relationship Data model.

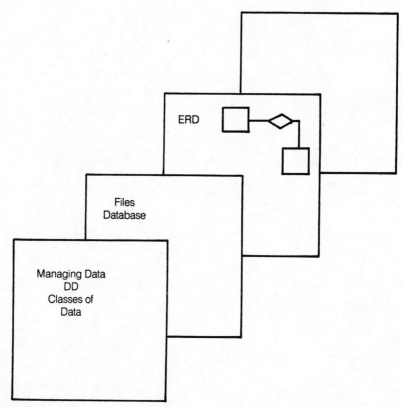

Figure 5.5. Overview-data management.

of data that is a part of a record. Data records are collections of data elements. Data stores are the files, temporary and permanent, or the database. The database was discussed briefly and also the relationship between data and files.

Entity Relationship Diagrams (ERD) were discussed to explain briefly the entity relationship for data in various files. An entity is the basic unit of information in the data dictionary.

Figure 5.5 depicts an overview of the main features of this chapter.

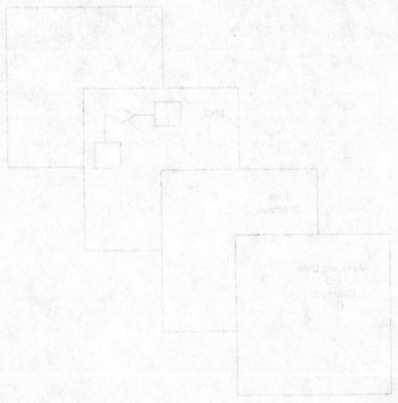

6

Logical Specifications

Logical specifications consist of brief descriptions of the processes described in an LDFD. They are also called miniature (mini) specifications and can be either narrative or concisely presented in structured English.

STRUCTURED ENGLISH

Structured English is a hybrid of the English language and a computer-logical language. The main features are:

- Imperative English verbs
- Terms from the data dictionary
- Reserved words to denote policy logic
- Simple sentences
- Precision
- Conciseness
- Use of graphics
- Maintainable system
- Tool for writing minispecs

An illustration of structured English is shown in Figure 6.1.

Mini Specifications Logic Blocks

Using these building blocks ensures that the mini specification can be read from beginning to end without forcing the reader to "go back" to amend his

```
For Each Employee-Record:
  Select Case Based On Payment-Type:
    Case 1:
      Weekly Salaried Employee
      If Hours-Worked Is Greater Than 40
        Regular-Hours Is Equal To 40
        Regular-Pay Is Equal To
          Regular-Hours Multiply By Regular-Wages
        Overtime-Hours Is Equal To
          Hours-Worked Minus 40
        Overtime-Pay Is Equal To
          Overtime-Hours Multiply By Overtime-Wage
        Gross-Pay Is Equal To Regular-Pay Plus
          Overtime-Pay
      ELSE
        Regular-Hours Is Equal To Hours-Worked
        Regular-Pay Is Equal To Regular-Hours
          Multiply By Regular-Wage
        Gross-Pay Is Equal To Regular-Pay
    Case 2:
      Biweekly Salaried Employee
      Gross-Pay Is Equal to Annual-Salary Divided by 26
```

Figure 6.1. Structured English minispec.

understanding of the policy. The logical building blocks are:

- sequence
- decision
- repetition

The blocks are illustrated in Figure 6.2.

Sample of Structured English Using Logic Blocks

```
SEQUENCE:
    REGULAR-PAY   = REGULAR-HOURS   × REGULAR-WAGE
    OVERTIME-PAY  = OVERTIME-HOURS  × OVERTIME-WAGE
    GROSS-PAY     = REGULAR-PAY     + OVERTIME-PAY

DECISION:
    IF EMPLOYEE-TYPE = "EXEMPT"
        OVERTIME-WAGE = REGULAR-WAGE
    ELSE
        OVERTIME-WAGE = REGULAR-WAGE × 2.0

REPETITION:
    FOR EACH PAYROLL-TRANSACTION:
        ISSUE PAY-STUB AND PAY-CHECK
```

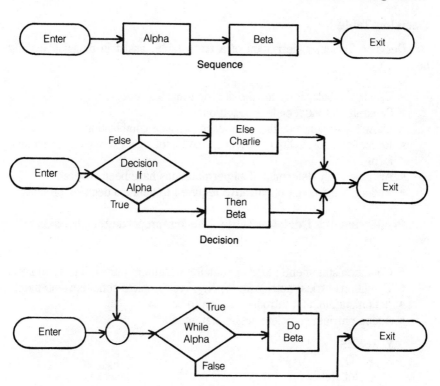

Figure 6.2. Logical blocks.

These specifications are just like algebraic equations. Remember, the names used are not used arbitrarily—they are already defined in data dictionary.

DECISION-ASSISTING DEVICES

Decision-assisting tools help you make decisions by:

- Reducing the possibility of information misinterpretation
- Determining if all permutations have been considered
- Reducing the amount of narrative text required to define a decision process.

The following are some of the many decision assisting tools available:

- Decision table
- Decision tree
- Decision graphics

Decision Table

Decision Tables, a derivation of a truth table, assist in decision making because they:

- Create a tabular form for the decision-making process
- Separate out independent conditions
- Show the action resulting from each possible combination
- Reduce the possibility of misinterpretation of logic expressed in narrative form
- Arithmetically determine if all permutations have been covered
- Reduce the amount of narrative required to define a decision process

Properties of a Decision Table. The four properties of a decision table are:

- Condition statements: kind of question statement introducing a condition
- Condition entries: entries in "Y, N, -" to complete condition statements
- Action statements: introduce action to be taken
- Action entries: complete action statements

Y = YES
N = NO
- = Not Related

Example. You are going to buy a new car. You approach a car dealer and after negotiation, finally decided to buy the car from him because he readily approved your credit and the car is suitable for your needs. While you are completing the necessary forms, the dealer quietly goes to the telephone and calls the credit bureau to check your credit.

He is making a decision on your credit report based on the following information:

- Credit is good
- Payments regular

Congratulations!!! The dealer has approved your credit to buy the car.
Solution. Credit approval procedure:

		R1	R2	R3	R4
C1	CREDIT IS OK	Y	Y	N	N
C2	SLOW PAYMENTS	Y	N	Y	N
A1	APPROVE CREDIT	N	Y	N	N

Here, C1 and C2 stand for conditions, A1 stands for action and R1, R2, R3, R4 stand for the rules of the decision table. Hence, the only "Y" is achieved when the credit is good and payments are regular.

Decision Tree

Decision trees are easy to read but may not be helpful in complicated situations. Some of the advantages are:

- Used to simplify structured-English when user's action depends on several variables
- A graphic tool
- More understandable
- User acceptable

To "read" a decision tree, start on the left and trace a path to the right, using the value of each condition to direct you along the appropriate branch of the tree.

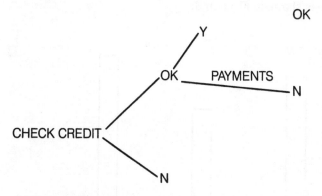

Decision Graphics

Graphics can display almost any type of comparative data on the screen. Since you specify the type of chart to create for each display, your data can be displayed in different formats for different situations. Charts are created by entering values in response to a series of screen prompts, and the chart is displayed instantly when all values have been keyed. If your chart is not what you expected, just revise it and redisplay. Once the charts are created, they may be printed by using the screen dump feature. You can also save a chart as a disk file for retrieval at a later time.

Most business graphics software can do almost everything a graphic artist can do by hand, and it can do it faster, more accurately, and with a greater variety of formats. Graphics can assist in decision making as much as tabular forms and data trees. Sometimes, their clarity makes them more effective for presentation.

The benefits of graphics as a decision assisting device are numerous because they are:

- Concise
- Clear
- A summarization
- Understandable
- Accurate
- Graphic representations

Types of Charts. There are three basic types of charts:

- Bar charts
- Line charts
- Pie charts

Bar Charts. Bar charts can display data as vertical bars on a graph. Bar charts are easy to use and understand and should never include more than seven bars. A sample is shown in Figure 6.3.

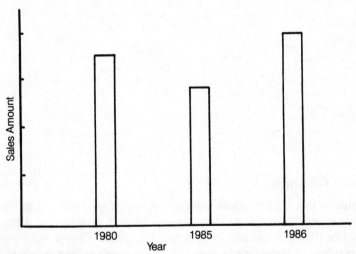

Figure 6.3. Bar Chart sample.

Line Chart. Line charts display data with straight lines that connect points on the graph, thereby showing relationships among various pieces of data. The number of line types is determined by how many topics the chart covers. A sample is shown in Figure 6.4.

Pie Chart. Pie charts display data as slices of a pie. The size of a slice indicates its relationship to the other slices and the whole pie. Ideally, a pie chart should have no more than five slices in order to keep it understandable. A sample is shown in Figure 6.5.

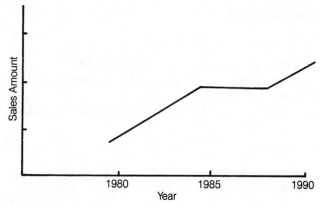

Figure 6.4. Line Chart sample.

Figure 6.5. Pie Chart sample.

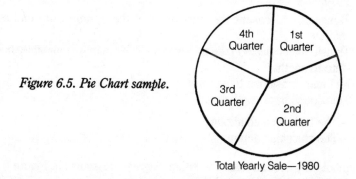

Most types of graphics can be drawn in three-dimensional space, and some can be rotated 360 degrees to have a complete, clear and better view of the data. Some of the advanced technologies that use graphics are:

- Laser screen display
- Ultralarge screen display
- Plasma display (medical)
- High-resolution video display
- Space probe picture relays

SYSTEM STATES TRANSITION DIAGRAM

A system state transition diagram (SSTD) is a depiction of possible states of the system, and at any given time, the system can be in only one of the states within the diagram. A state has a unique combination of conditions and destinations in a system. Input information received by the system defines the movement from state to state. An SSTD provides a complete picture of the effect of input data on system processing, and therefore enhances the visibility of the information flow through the system.

Thus, to summarize:

- SSTDs depict a state of a system

  – A state is a mode of behavior of the system
  – A state is a particular set of behaviors that has a unique combination of conditions and destinations
  – At any given time, a system can be in only *one* of the states on a system state transition diagram

- Initial state

  – Active state
  – Indicated by double-headed arrow

- Final state

  – No outgoing transitions

- Transitions represent the movement of the system from one state to another
- Transitions (logically) take no time; the system moves instantly from one state to another
- Multiple transitions to and from a given state are permissible
- Transitions have two parts:

  – The transition condition
  – The transition action

Symbols of a system state transition diagram are shown in Figure 6.6. Guidelines for drawing an SSTD:

- Compile an event list
- Identify relationships among the events
- Group related events—sequences, loops, mutual exclusivity, independence
- Introduce transition conditions and actions
- Fill up state names
- Add control signals between sets of states
- Use process projections to fill up any gap

A sample SSTD is shown in Figure 6.7.

SUMMARY

We discussed in this chapter the minispecs for defining a process, component and unit. We also defined Structured English. Decision assisting devices were discussed, along with decision tables and decision trees, and decision graphics like bar, line, and pie charts were illustrated. Finally, SSTDs were discussed.

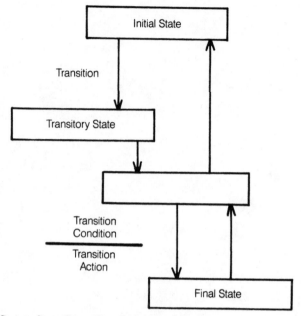

Figure 6.6. System State Transition Diagram symbols.

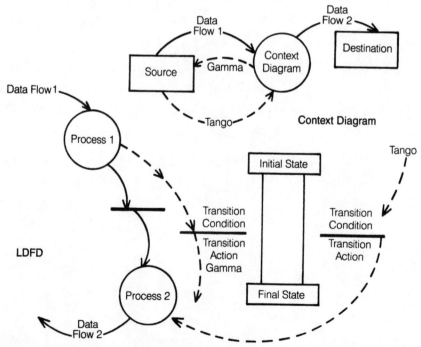

Figure 6.7. System State Transition Diagram sample.

7

System Logical Design

The purpose of a system logical design (SLD) phase is to translate the customer-oriented functional specifications, which were identified in Chapter 4 and documented in Chapters 5 and 6, into a set of computer-oriented technical specifications to confirm the programs or computer system component items.

The logical system flow, logical data organization, inputs/outputs and related logical specification were described in Chapters 4, 5 and 6 to satisfy the customer. In the SLD phase, the same will be confirmed to satisfy the computer. Moreover, the computer system design will develop the internal view of the system.

The independent functions defined and analyzed in the system logical requirements analysis phase will be allocated to the "system top-level" modular design, which is also called system preliminary design. This phase confirms the system components, units and modules and is based on the allocation of specific requirements to individual functional areas. It is not always easy to find an executive to control other component items. Sometimes, it is easy to create a new *executive*, or control module, to take charge of all the controls, switches and timing frequency.

The SLD phase also assesses the risk involved in putting an independent function into a particular component, along with the practicality of the implementation solution. These tools will help system reliability and ease of maintenance.

The objectives of this phase are to determine a technical design suitable to support the data and processing requirements which will meet timeliness, accuracy and performance criteria.

TOP-LEVEL SYSTEM STRUCTURED DESIGN

Top-level modular design of each computer system component item will be defined as it incorporates and reflects the independent functions, related files and data flows inputs/outputs. The requirements are then more completely decomposed and allocated to the proper function of the associated computer software component. The design can be derived from various levels of logical data flow diagrams.

When a logical computer software component has been defined, the requirement is further decomposed in accordance with the leveling of an LDFD and allocated to a functional unit performing the required processing. Finally, the requirement is allocated to the module in the unit that performs the required action to produce the desired result.

The top-level system design technique ensures that each independent function acts in response to the requirement which has been thoroughly analyzed in system logical requirements analysis and incorporated in an LDFD at various levels. Each of these independent functions is traceable to a top-level software component.

Hierarchical Levels

The levels of functional hierarchy correspond to levels of control of the task to be performed by the system—this is practically a transliteration of LDFD levels into system design levels. The top level contains the highest level of control logic within the software hierarchy. A sample of a structured chart is shown in Figure 7.1.

Each level of the hierarchy consists of software modules whose operations are subordinate to the software modules in the next highest level. These are represented by rectangles or squares.

It is not always easy to find the highest level module from the LDFD. Sometimes, it is more convenient to create a new module—called "executive"—which will control other sub-modules. An example is shown in Figure 7.2 (please refer to the LDFD in Chapter 4's case study).

Distinct Computer Programs

A program is commonly called a computer software configuration item (CSCI) and it consists of one or more computer software components (CSC). A computer software component consists of one or more units, and a unit consists of one or more modules. The purpose of this design phase is to decompose a computer system into the same module levels as were arrived at in the system requirement logical analysis phase. The difference is that we are reconfirming what we have already identified.

At the same time, we can visualize the system concept of decomposition into components, modules and units, which will present us with the clear pic-

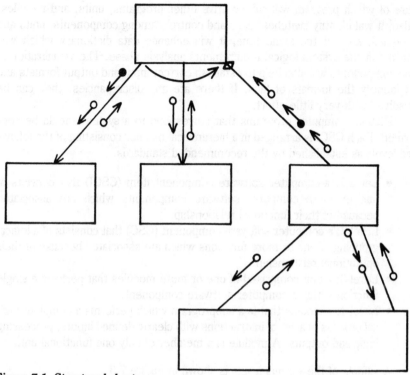

Figure 7.1. Structured chart.

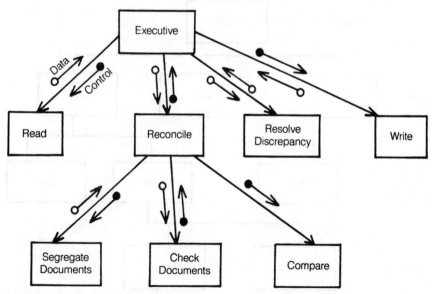

Figure 7.2. Structured chart sample.

ture of which program will call or drive other programs, units, and modules. Also, it will identify switches, flags and controls among components, units and modules, and, at the same time, it will enhance data dictionary which was started at the system logical requirements analysis phase. The visualization of the components will also help to establish correct input and output formats and to identify the formats of files. If there are any discrepancies, they can be resolved with very little effort.

Distinct computer programs that correspond to a system should be confirmed. Each CSCI is arranged in a hierarchical manner consisting of the following levels as established by the recommended standards.

- Level 1: a computer software component item (CSCI) that consists of one or more computer software components which are associated because of their functional relationship.
- Level 2: a computer software component (CSC) that consists of a logical grouping of one or more functions which are associated because of their operational relationship.
- Level 3: a unit comprised of one or more modules that perform a single function within a computer software component.
- Level 4: a module that is a subprogram which performs a complete logical process of a set of instructions with clearly defined inputs, processing logic and outputs. A module is a member of only one functional unit.

A sample of the various levels is shown in Figure 7.3.

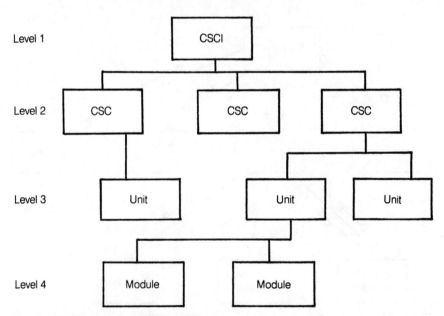

Figure 7.3. Distinct computer programs.

Each module's structure conforms to the following conventions:

- Consists of a set of contiguous program instructions in a form acceptable to a computer and having a name by which other modules may invoke it
- Is limited to about 100 source instructions in length, excluding commentary
- Contains a single entry/exit statement
- Has a distinct set of variable names
- Has good inter-dependent coupling between a module, unit and component with strong cohesion among them
- Confirms factors of LDFD
- Can share common functions such as updating, etc. among others, executive/calling modules, units and components

Efficient Techniques for a System Design

Structured charts are drawn to identify system items, components, units and modules, and are direct translations of LDFD's, in addition to any other utility needed to be included in the system. The system design can be made more efficient by observing the following features:

- Each component, unit and module is coupled properly with each other without redundancy
- Each component, unit and module can be coded independently without any clash of interest with others
- The sublevels are named properly
- The common routines are labeled well
- Refine the system design to eliminate any redundancy
- Modify LDFD's, if need be, with respect to the changes made in the system design

Controls/Switches

Controls and switches are represented by an arrow with a solid dot. At the top-level modular system design, the goal is to identify how the other components, units and modules are being accessed, controlled and executed with the help of controls and switches. They are different than data, which is represented by an arrow with a small circle. The objective of controls and switches in all the levels is to identify the flow of data between components under certain conditions.

OBJECT-ORIENTED DESIGN

Object-oriented design decomposes a system upon the concept of an object which is an entity whose behavior is characterized by the actions that it requires of other objects. Such a design has the added benefits of producing reusable software components and the ability to use existing reusable components. Most importantly, object-oriented design maps well with Ada and exploits the power of Ada.

According to the Abbot and Booch theory, the following steps are used in deriving object-oriented design:

- Identify the objects
- Identify the operations suffered by and required of each object
- Establish the visibility of each object in relation to other objects
- Establish the interface of each object
- Implement each object

Advantages

- Useful at high-level design
- Maps well with Ada
- Exploits the power of Ada
- Ada/PDL follows right away from the preliminary design to the implementation phase

Disadvantages

- Not very useful at lower level of design
- Restricted to a few coding languages

DATA STRUCTURED DESIGN

Data structured design focuses on the data of a problem. The data structures are defined first and then the architecture of the system is based on those data structures, according to the Jackson, Warnier theory.

Advantages

- Recommended for COBOL
- Concentrate on data
- Treat operations in a global fashion
- Useful for subprograms

Disadvantages

- Restricted applications

DEVELOP A SYSTEM SOFTWARE TEST PROCEDURE

You must plan and define the test procedures and techniques that will help to verify the software development in the later phases. You can then verify the completeness and correctness of the implementation of the software development. Test planning should be conducted concurrently with the system development and the following parameters should be defined:

- Requirements of testing
- Performance of testing
- Test data
- Files
- Schedules
- Sequences
- Interfaces
- Error recovery
- Verification of the results
- Structured walk-throughs
- Operational procedures
- Test levels
- Test cases

PLAN A SYSTEM SOFTWARE ACCEPTANCE PROCEDURE

The final objective of software development is that it should be accepted by the customer. Therefore, it is advisable to plan the acceptance procedures at this phase. Such plans should be agreed upon by the customer. The following activities may help:

- Discussion of the criteria to be used for acceptance by the customer
- Planning methods to conduct the acceptance testing
- Scheduling for preparation of the acceptance tests
- Identification of resources available for the acceptance tests
- Identification of available personnel skills
- Organization to conduct the acceptance tests

PRODUCTS OF SYSTEM LOGICAL DESIGN

The result of software preliminary design is to produce the following documents:

- Structured charts
- Related specifications

- Updated data dictionary
- Updated files (DB)
- Updated logical specifications
- Updated LDFD
- Input/output formats
- Initiating test plans
- Structured walk-through reports and summary
- Reviews showing that the logical system design (top-level) satisfies the software requirements allocated from the higher-level documents

SUMMARY

We discussed structured chart diagrams which allow the software designer to identify components of a system. These diagrams are directly translated from the data flow diagram. The decomposition of components to unit and module levels reflects exactly the leveling and partitioning schema of data flow diagram, and the name of the components, units and modules are consistent with the data dictionary. We also identified the need to select an executive to control the decomposed components.

We discussed how Jackson also developed structure diagrams like the structured charts. The difference is that, in a structured diagram, each operation is defined more precisely—as sequential, conditional or iterative. These types of operations are indicated by symbols.

- a sequential operation is shown as a rectangle
- a conditional operation is shown as a box with a zero (0) above the upper right-hand corner
- an iterative operation is depicted by a box with an asterisk (*) above the upper right-hand corner

A sample structure diagram is shown in Figure 7.4. Several more symbols have been developed to support the programming techniques.

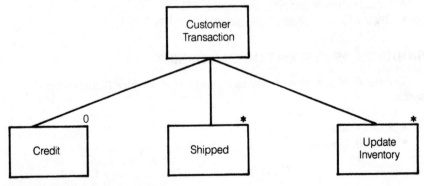

Figure 7.4. Structure diagram.

A CSCI sample static structure of DOD-STD-2167A is shown in Figure 7.5 which illustrates another system of decomposing a computer software configuration item into top-level computer software components (TLCSC), lower-level computer software components (LLCSC) and units.

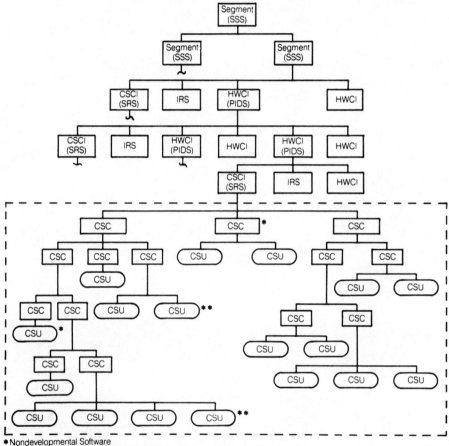

* Nondevelopmental Software
**Same CSU Used by Different CSCs

Figure 7.5. System breakdown and CSCI organization structure.

Section III
Computer Systems Software Development and Implementation Techniques

8

Program Logical Design

The design of each computer software component and its modules is generated to the point where it can be coded in a suitable language. This is also called program detailed design. The logical detailed design is defined in a manner to allow for coding and may need logical flow charting for complex modules, units and components which will reflect the required specifications. There are many techniques available for logical flow charting. A few will be discussed, including:

- Top-down concept
- Logical flow chart
- Program design language
- HIPO
- NS chart
- Pseudo code
- IF—THEN—ELSE statements
- Nested IF—THEN—ELSE statements

TOP-DOWN CONCEPT

The top-down concept is the structured approach to drawing the program flow chart. The levels of the program functional hierarchy correspond to levels of control of the tasks to be performed by the computer software component, units and modules. The top level contains the highest level of control logic within the CSC software program hierarchy. A sample of a VTOC (Visual Table Of Contents), which illustrates the hierarchy, is shown in Figure 8.1. Each level of the hierarchy consists of CSC program software functions whose operations are subordinated to the program instructions in the next highest level. This

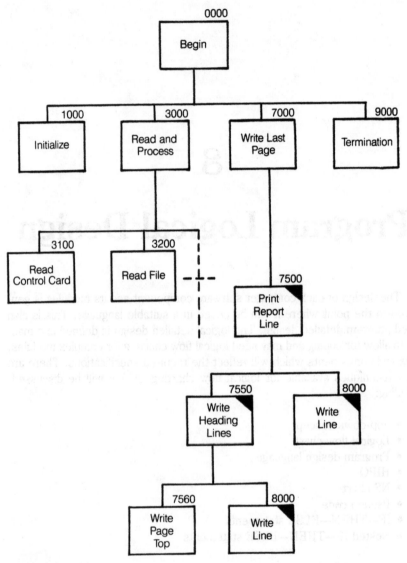

Figure 8.1. VTOC.

structure is based upon the Constantine and Yourdon methods. The various levels are represented as rectangles or squares that are consistently numbered and named and that correspond to the numbers and names on the system structured chart, which further correspond to the same entity in the logical data flow diagram.

Most of the program functions which are repeated can be shown with black on the upper right-hand corner, rather than to show them again and again, making the flow chart complicated.

Advantages

- State-of-the-art technique
- Uniformity
- Follows structured techniques
- Well documented
- Easy to follow
- Easy to draw
- Easy to understand
- Can be automated

Disadvantages

- Relatively new concept in the computer industry
- Decisions are not shown clearly

LOGICAL FLOW CHART

Logical flow charts are a conventional technique and have existed since the inception of computer industry. The blocks are represented according to template figures with most of the functional actions represented in conventional diagrams such as:

- Decision—diamond shape
- Start/stop—cylinder
- Input/output process—parallelogram
- Computation process—rectangle
- Magnetic tape
- Connector
- Display
- Magnetic drum
- Off-page connector

Also, a set of conventions are defined to place a number of subroutines on a page. The logic flow chart relates to the coding source listings, and the logic flow language is a program design language which can be translated into structured code. A sample logical flow chart is shown in Figure 8.2.

A set of flow standards can be established, including:

- Two columns per line
- Five or seven boxes vertical per page
- Entries from the left
- Exits from the right
- Flow from top to bottom
- Lines not crossing
- No confusion in labeling and naming

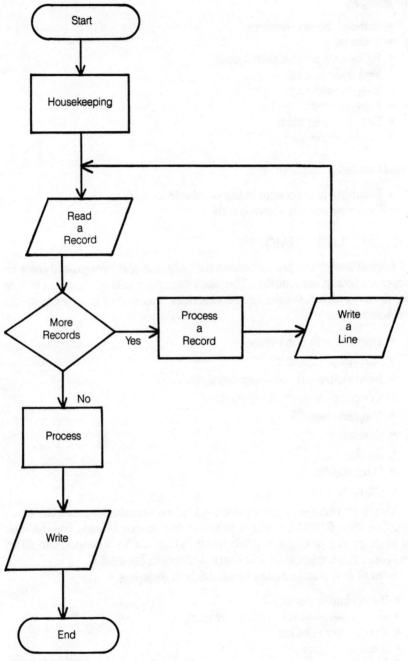

Figure 8.2. Flow chart.

Advantages

- Conventional technique
- Has been in practice since the inception of computer industry

Disadvantages

- Lack of numbering system
- Lack of naming convention
- Connectivity problem
- Not structured
- Difficult to follow
- Difficult to understand

PROGRAM DESIGN LANGUAGE

Program design language (PDL) is one of the best detailed design tools available today. A PDL represents the internal logic of a component, unit and module that is easy for a programmer to understand and write. Its purpose is to improve communications among software designers, programmers and managers through the use of commonly understood terms and concepts.

A PDL is based on a particular language used for coding the detailed design. For example, a PDL based on Ada constructs an Ada/PDL which is compilable in order to keep code and design together and to let the language check for logical inconsistencies. It also supports the use of reusable software components. The PDL should be formal, to allow automatic processing, and should include all of Ada, plus extensions to provide the capability for tools which aid in documentation and management.

PDL is a set of textual, English-like structured expressions that consists of the English language, a computer language or a combination of the two.

Advantages

- Easy to understand
- Easy to follow
- Easy to adopt with a coding language
- Easy to document
- Can be automated

Disadvantages

- Fairly new tool in the market
- Language oriented

HIPO

The HIPO (Hierarchy plus Input-Process-Output) displays the input to the program. The technique uses the process to input data, and the format of the output results. It predicts the different stages of the program, while explaining the input, process and output. A sample is shown in Figure 8.3.

HIPO can be prepared as follows:

- Fill up the heading
- Start filling up the output
- Figures can be shown to represent tapes, files
- Storage areas can be shown
- Fill up the corresponding input
- Identify the process linking input and corresponding output
- Arrows can be drawn to connect the path of input, process and output

Advantages
- Displays input, process and output formats
- Good tool for a complicated system

Disadvantages
- Laborious
- Requires a lot of paperwork

NS CHARTS

Nassi-Shneiderman (NS) Charts or Chapin Charts represent visibility of control logic, and they guarantee structured code for one module, unit or component. A sample is shown in Figure 8.4.

PSEUDO CODE

Pseudo code is considered a detailed design language that is compatible with any coding language. It looks like Structured English but is geared more toward coding, but it is an informal coding language not intended to be executed on a computer. Its purpose is to organize a programmer's thoughts prior to coding. A sample of a COBOL language pseudo code is presented in Figure 8.5.

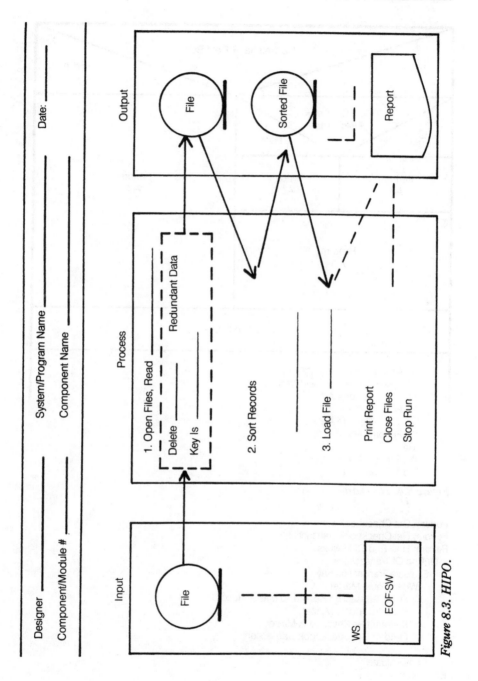

Figure 8.3. HIPO.

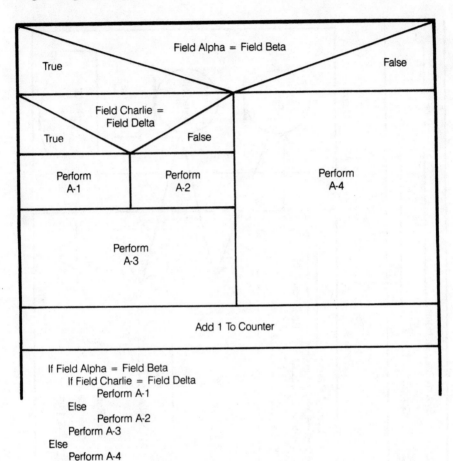

```
If Field Alpha = Field Beta
    If Field Charlie = Field Delta
            Perform A-1
    Else
            Perform A-2
    Perform A-3
Else
    Perform A-4
Add 1 To Counter
```

Figure 8.4. NS chart.

```
Perform Get-Checkbook-Master
Perform Get-Checkbook-Transaction
Perform Until End-Of-Masters
    Or End-Of-Transactions
    Evaluate Transaction-Key
        When Equal Master-Key
            Move Transaction Record To Master-Record
            Perform Update-Master
            Perform Get-Checkbook-Master
            Perform Get-Checkbook-Transaction
            . . . . . . . . . . . . . . . . . . . . .
    End-Evaluate
End-Perform
```

Figure 8.5. Pseudo code.

116

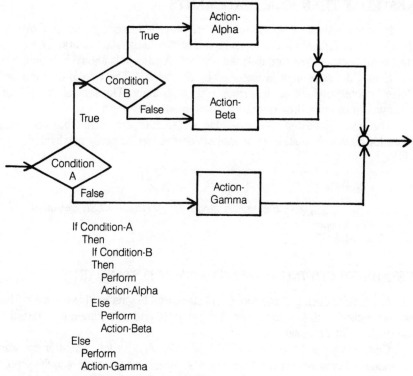

```
If Condition-A
   Then
      If Condition-B
      Then
         Perform
         Action-Alpha
      Else
         Perform
         Action-Beta
   Else
      Perform
      Action-Gamma
```

Figure 8.6. Nested IF—THEN—ELSE.

Advantages

- Easy to follow
- Easy to understand
- Can be automated
- Language oriented
- Can easily translate into COBOL 85
- Good tool for a fresh programmer

Disadvantages
- Needs extra step for translating from pseudo to old COBOL

IF-THEN-ELSE STATEMENTS

If—then—else statements involve a condition test for either a true or false statement that can be followed by the execution of a process. A sample is shown in Figure 8.6.

NESTED IF-THEN-ELSE STATEMENTS

Nested if—then—else statements are so-called because one or more if—then—else statements are contained within the initial statements. The entire statement is called "nested if—then—else". A sample is shown in Figure 8.7.

Each "if" statement is matched by an "else." The rule is that the first "else" corresponds to the innermost "if" statement. The second "else" corresponds to the next innermost "if" statement, and so on.

The level of nested if—then—else statements should not be more than three for clarity. A multi-level nested statement can be easily subdivided.

```
If Condition 1
  If Condition 2
    If Condition 3
      Else Perform A
    Else Perform B
  Else Perform C
```

Figure 8.7. Nested IF—THEN—ELSE statement.

ESTABLISH CODING CONVENTIONS AND STANDARDS

Planning of coding conventions and standards begins in Phase 1 when they are reconciled with the customer requirements and sometimes committed to the request for proposal.

Conventions and standards should provide security for computer software component items and related documents, which means they should protect codes, data, test data, source code and object code listings. A password is used to access the documents by authorized personnel and any encryption techniques used are to safeguard the documents. Proper backup procedures should be clarified to save the data in case any mishap occurs during execution.

The top-down approach should be used to develop the software while the bottom-up approach can be used to test the modules, units and components. The effect of memory crunch must be identified. Gather the appropriate coding language manuals since high order language (HOL) should be used wherever possible and permissible. Names of data variables must be recorded in the DATA DICTIONARY if they are not already included. Module, unit, component, item, subroutine, label and table names should be adhered to within the data dictionary. Any new element's name should be meaningful, unique and in accordance with the established standards and conventions.

Structuring data should be enlisted in the data dictionary, and only files registered in the database should be accessed. Any new tables or arrays should be set up in accordance with the established standards and conventions.

A structured coding approach should be followed; this makes the coding easy to understand. Structured walk-throughs should be encouraged at all levels of coding, and all the walk-throughs and other events should be properly recorded. Comments should be used extensively throughout coding; the linkage routine should be properly documented.

Develop Test Plans

Test plans should be developed to test modules, units, components, items or system integration. (These plans have been initiated at previous phases.) Standards test files should be provided with test data for testing at various stages; it is important to standardize to compare the test results. Test tools should be used for tracing and snapshot dumps.

Input/Output Formats

Input/output formats should be clearly defined for each module, unit and component and fully recorded in the data dictionary. Each should include diagnostic and failsafe logic with intermediate results as well as final outputs. Data should be easily readable for input and output and it should be labelled for input, output and input/output with consistency to the data dictionary. Avoid complicated calculations; they can always be converted into simple subroutines.

Report Formats

Report formats can be standardized by putting the first two lines with standardized headings in the center of the format. The end of page can be labeled, and the subtotals or totals can be properly formatted. The last page and the first page of the report can be properly designed.

PRODUCTS OF PROGRAM LOGICAL DESIGN

The following documents are generated as the development of the design proceeds:

- Module data dictionary—data dictionary is enhanced with the unfolding of each module into detailed logical design for coding
- Module database files layouts—database file layouts are identified and defined
- Module flow diagrams—modules are logically flow-charted prior to encoding
- Establish documents like software development files (SDF)—These documents are initiated for each module/unit and enhanced as the software development progresses
- Document all records and reports about structured walk-throughs to ensure error-free modules and units and logical flow charting
- Man-machine and others inter-operability interfaces are conducted
- An audit trail is established to satisfy the customer about the system software's successful achievements up to this phase and to plan for implementation in the future

SUMMARY

We discussed in this chapter many topics, such as top-down, conventional flow chart, PDL, pseudo code, HIPO, NS chart, if—then—else, and Nested if—then—else statements. We learned to establish standards and conventions for coding and discussed the development of test plans. Finally, we discussed the products of logical design.

9

Computer Systems Implementation

Computer systems implementation consists of a unit/module coding and testing phase, a computer software component testing phase and a system integration testing phase. Finally the system software can be documented and placed into production and accepted by the customer.

CODING LANGUAGES

The program detailed design is coded into the desired language—there are many languages available in the computer industry. (The decisions about the language and type of computer are made much earlier during the requirements phase.) Now is the time when detailed designs of each component, unit and module is handed over to the team of programmers whose job it is to code the various activities into the desired language.

The code is compiled, executed and validated as the system software. The documents mentioned in the earlier phases are updated by the programmer team, and internal module and unit tests and integration tests are conducted and documented to ensure that the requirements have been implemented to achieve desired results.

Leaders of the coding teams must perform preliminary work in establishing the environment and work areas for programmers. Proper documentations, standards, libraries, establishing of account numbers, suitable training and guidance should be provided to the programmers.

The following steps should be defined when coding any computer program:

- Input data
- Files and records consisting of the data

- Switches and controls
- Data accessing techniques
- Output formats
- Logic for processing the data
- Save input data
- Save output
- Documentation
- Brief functional comments for each coded instruction

A sample program in COBOL is illustrated in Figure 9.1. Please refer to Figure 8.1 for a top-down sample.

UNIT/MODULE TESTING

The programmers conduct the unit tests, and a code walk-through is conducted for each unit/module before testing. Tests are conducted for all coded modules, units and components.

These tests consist of:

- Static testing
- Desk checking
- Code walk-through
- Dynamic testing which exercises actual operation of individual unit/module
- Establish test file sources
- Create test sequence
- Prepare test data
- Compile and execute test
- Analyze test report
- Correct errors and retest

All successful tests results are documented in the SDF for reference and records.

A summarization of testing is illustrated in Figure 9.2.

COMPUTER SOFTWARE COMPONENT TESTING

The integration testing of the system software is conducted to verify usefulness, viability and requirements compliance of all the CSC software composing the CSCI. This phase is composed of a series of tests used to demonstrate that the system software performs the desired requirements and is ready for formal review and extensive testing.

Functional integration testings are conducted extensively at the informal level; these tests ensure that module and unit levels testing is successful. CSCs

IDENTIFICATION DIVISION.
PROGRAM-ID.   meaningful name of a unit/module/component.
AUTHOR.   (Your name).
INSTALLATION.   (name of your office).
DATE-WRITTEN.   MM/YY.
DATE-COMPILED.   today date.
REMARKS.   (a comprehensive description of the program's
                    functions which may include:
                        job work order number
                        general description
                        inputs
                        outputs
                        files accessing techniques
                        – sequential
                        – random
                        sort procedures and accessing keys
                        processing techniques
                        detail about revision/version

ENVIRONMENT DIVISION.
*
CONFIGURATION SECTION.

SOURCE-COMPUTER.   computer name.
OBJECT-COMPUTER.   computer name.

SPECIAL-NAMES.   if any.
*
INPUT-OUTPUT   SECTION.

FILE-CONTROL.
        SELECT .... FILE
            ASSIGN TO UT-S-XXXXXXXX.

DATA DIVISION.
*
FILE SECTION.
*
FD .... FILE
        LABEL RECORDS ARE STANDARD
        BLOCK CONTAINS 0 RECORDS.
01 -------- RECORD   PICTURE X( ).

        ----

*
FD   :
*   :
SD   SORT-FILE.
        05   SORT-KEY   PICTURE X( ).
        05   FILLER   PICTURE X( ).
*
WORKING-STORAGE SECTION.
the first entry in working storage should start with level 77.

77 ----------   PICTURE X( ).
77   ----------   PICTURE X( )   VALUE
                                        ZEROS
        all other entries should be grouped together under 01,
such as switches, flags, control fields, counters,
subscripts, tables, report headings.....

```
01   ALL-COUNTERS.
     05   COUNTER-1              PICTURE S9(5)   COMP-3.
               --------------------

01   ALL- .......
     05   --------              PICTURE    ...
                                    VALUE ZEROS.

          10   .........        PICTURE  ...
               15   ......      PICTURE  ...
     PROCEDURE DIVISION.
```

the first paragraph should always look like this in the same order.
This has the same number and names as has been defined on the
VTOC and HIPO or any other form of detailed design.

```
     0000- BEGIN.
          PERFORM 1000-INITIALIZE.
          PERFORM 3000-READ-AND-PROCESS.
          PERFORM 7000-WRITE-LAST-PAGE.
          PERFORM 9000-TERMINATE.
          STOP RUN.
```

if EXIT are used, rewrite the above paragraph, such as,

```
          PERFORM 1000-INITIALIZE THRU 1000-EXIT.
          PERFORM 3000-READ-AND-PROCESS THRU 3000-EXIT.
          PERFORM 7000-WRITE-LAST-PAGE THRU 7000-EXIT.
          PERFORM 9000-TERMINATION THRU 9000-EXIT.
          STOP RUN.
     1000-INITIALIZE.
          DISPLAY "PROGRAM-NAME COMPILED "   DATE-COMPILED.
          OPEN INPUT
               .......
               OUTPUT
          MOVE SPACES TO    .....
     1000-EXIT.
          EXIT.
     3000-READ-AND-PROCESS.
          PERFORM 3100-READ-CONTROL-CARD.
          PERFORM 3200-READ-FILE ------.
               ..........
               ..........
          PERFORM 3500-READ-FILEX -----
               UNTIL   EOF-SW = 'Y'.
                    .
                    .
                    .
                    .
     3100-READ-CONTROL-CARD.
               :
     3200-READ-FILE-----.
               .
          PAGE EJECT
     7000-WRITE-LAST-PAGE.
          PERFORM 7500-PRINT-REPORT-LINE.
               :
```

```
7500-PRINT-REPORT-LINE.
    IF COUNT-LINE > 55
        MOVE 0 TO COUNT-LINE
        PERFORM 7550-WRITE-HEADING-LINES.
    PERFORM 8000-WRITE-LINE.

7550-WRITE-HEADING-LINES.
    ADD 1 TO COUNT-PAGE.
    ⋮

    PERFORM 7560-WRITE-PAGE-TOP.

7560-WRITE-PAGE-TOP.
    ⋮

8000-WRITE-LINE.
    WRITE REPORT-LINE.
    MOVE SPACES TO REPORT-LINE.
    ADD 1 TO COUNT-LINE.
    ⋮


9000-TERMINATE.

    CLOSE FILES ----
            ------
            -----

    DISPLAY "NUMBER OF INPUT RECORD READ = " INPUT-CNT.
    DISPLAY "NUMBER OF RECORDS WRITTEN = " OUTPUT-CNT.


    ⋮

    DISPLAY "PROGRAM NAME RUNS SUCCESSFULLY".

9000-EXIT.
    EXIT.
```

Figure 9.1. A Cobol Program.

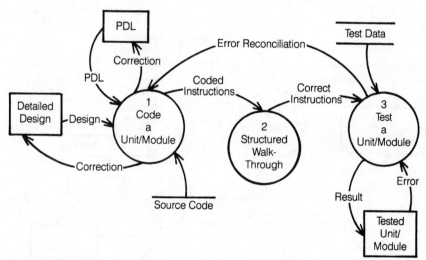

Figure 9.2. Unit testing scheme.

are integrated individually in a top-down manner to demonstrate their correctness and interfacing capability; these tests verify that the software design and performance satisfy the requirements of the software specifications.

Functional thread analysis is conducted to identify all functions along the functional thread plus the corresponding partial software system needed for testing these functions. A functional allocation matrix is utilized to identify and integrate the unit and CSCs necessary to implement and test a particular software requirement function. All functions that successfully pass functional thread testing are then submitted for acceptance testing. Changes made to any module after passing the test necessitate the retesting of all elements on the functional thread.

The following activities are conducted during testing:

- Prepare CSC test data
- Compile and execute test
- Verify test report
- Correct errors and retest

CSC integration testing is illustrated in Figure 9.3.

SYSTEM INTEGRATION TESTING

The CSCI integrates all CSCs in the system for formal validation testing that is conducted by an outside agency chosen by the customer. This testing will verify the system functions as designed and implemented. The system software

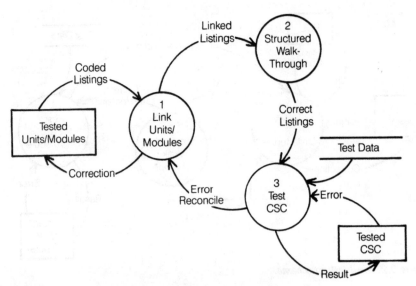

Figure 9.3. Computer Software Component testing illustration.

development team cooperates with and assists the outsiders conducting the tests. The following documents will be produced by the outsider responsible for the formal testing of the integrated system:

- Records and summary reports of internal reviews conducted
- Software test reports for the CSCI testing
- Interoperability with other systems
- Interfaces with other systems
- Verification of test output

The system integration testing is illustrated in Figure 9.4.

SYSTEM DOCUMENTATION

The following documents will be produced for the system:

- Records and summary of all the internal reviews conducted
- Source and object code listings for all software
- Any job control language listing needed for testing
- Updated design documentations
- Update SDFs
- Detailed test procedures for conducting each informal CSC integration test, including the test cases
- Software product specification for each CSCI
- System user manuals
- Audit reports to demonstrate CSCI was successfully tested and meets the requirements as described by the customer

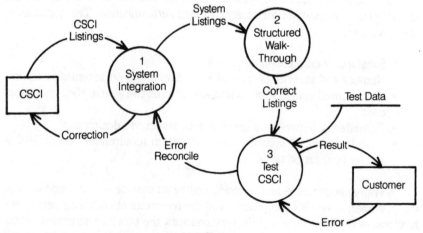

Figure 9.4. System integration testing illustration.

- Software test reports
- Copy/call members
- Utility/sort control cards
- Test data files
- Installation manuals

SYSTEM PRODUCTIVITY

The purpose of the system productivity phase is to verify that the system is doing what it is supposed to and that the customer is satisfied with its operability and results. The plans should be scheduled to initiate the system in production. The following activities will be conducted:

- Develop procedures and manuals for customer
- Print system guide for customer
- Plan to educate and train customer about the system
- Prepare customer data, input master files
- Install the system on customer computer
- Compile and test with actual customer data
- Create outputs for customer
- Check for accuracy and validity of output results
- Check data entry procedures

The final task is to turn the system to regular production. At that point, the project software development phases are completed.

ACCEPTANCE BY THE CUSTOMER

All updated and approved system documents and the system software are submitted to the customer for acceptance and authentication. The documentation consist of:

- Satisfactory completion of all audits
- Number and severity of unresolved software and documentation errors
- Documented evidence of correlation between the source code and object code
- Consistency between the code and its associated documents
- Certification of compliance with the system requirements as defined in the request for proposal

A system acceptance test is conducted by an outside agency appointed by the customer. It verifies compliance with the requirements of the system specifications, with the system architecture and with the other requirements documented in the Request For Proposal. The final acceptance is based upon the results obtained during the acceptance tests and the results of the audits reports.

EVALUATION

An evaluation of the technical achievements of the system and the performance of the system management team must be conducted by an independent team of computer professionals. The purpose of the evaluation is to determine if the system was developed in accordance with the established methodology.

If, during the course of system development, some lessons were learned, they may be helpful in the future bidding of a proposal, and the following was achieved:

- Team met the cost
- Performance achieved in time
- System qualitative productivity
- Proper technical methodology followed
- Future recommendations to save cost and time realized
- Future course of actions for improvements charted
- The system meets RFP
- Efficiency of system development team improved
- Proper documentations carried out
- Customer satisfied

At this point, future plans and actions are recommended on the basis of achievements. A report is written and submitted including:

- Planning
- Recommendations
- Findings
- Budgeting
- Scheduling
- Technical performance
- Management performance
- Cost effectiveness

SUMMARY

In this chapter, we have learned some coding techniques such as, structured, readable, understandable, and traceable techniques.

We learned that unit testing is very important. You can relate it with the foundation of a building: if the foundation of a building is strong, the building will last longer.

We also discussed the CSC and system integration testing along with the importance of well-designed documentations. Finally, we outlined acceptance of

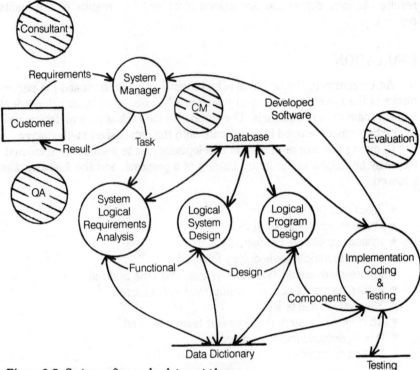

Figure 9.5. System software development phases.

the system by the customer, and learned that evaluation of the system software development and its performance is vital for learning about and correcting mistakes in the future.

An overview of the chapter is illustrated in Figure 9.5.

Section *IV*
Computer Systems Life-Cycle Software Maintenance Techniques

10

Computer Systems Software Maintenance

Once a computer-developed system is in production, it needs to be maintained for efficient results. Software maintenance requires good structured tools, effective communication among workers for increased productivity and low expenses. The cost of computer software development is growing every year and, with it, the cost of maintenance is accelerating, as shown in Figure 10.1. The price of computer software maintenance increases sharply when the system software is not developed with the proper methodology and documentation.

TYPES OF COMPUTER SYSTEM SOFTWARE

Types of computer system software have developed as structured or unstructured, as described in Figure 10.2.

Structured Computer System Software

Most of the computer systems (in the 1980s) are developing with a suitable methodology, which is already dictated by the RFP or computer system requirements. Today's systems have all the necessary documentation for the customer to maintain the system with more ease and less expense. A sample of a structured methodology is illustrated in Figure 10.3.

Unstructured Computer System Software

However, there are computer systems software which were developed in 60's and 70's that are hard to maintain. Some of the maintenance problems are

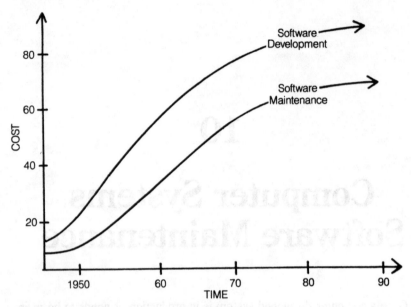

Figure 10.1. Computer systems cost trend.

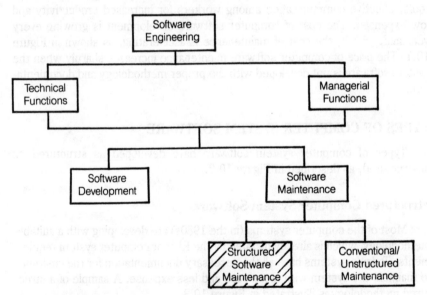

Figure 10.2. Types of computer system software.

that the systems were developed without:

- Structure
- Methodology

- Proper documentation
- System model
- Tools for maintenance
- Procedures or standards for maintenance

These systems may still be productive, but are not:

- Reliable
- Productive
- Manageable
- Maintainable

The system developers were rushed to finish their jobs. Errors were left to be detected and corrected at the end of the job, and the systems were never planned well for development and maintenance.

Example

Using a primitive computer systems software can be compared to maintaining a five-story building having 300 rooms but no blueprints. You are asked to go to the fifth floor, but given no directions. You get lost (or exhausted) after walking through all of the 100 rooms on the first floor to find the steps to go to the second floor. And once you are on the second floor, you have to go through the 85 rooms there to find the steps to go to the third floor. You face the same problems passing through 65 rooms on the third floor and the forty nine rooms on the fourth floor. You finally reach the fifth floor, and it has only 1 executive room.

Now, if the same people give you the clear directions to get you to the fifth floor by telling you to go to certain rooms on the first, second, third, fourth and fifth floors, and they guide you well with proper documentation and graphics (maps) so that you can understand the directions, you will happily reach the fifth floor and in much less time. In turn, you would be happy to maintain such a building. The second system is called the structured approach, and the same analogy applies in maintaining a computer system.

WHY MAINTENANCE IS SO EXPENSIVE

The expense algorithm depends upon the following factors:

- Set up an organization to maintain the system
- To understand the existing system
- To educate about the functionality of the system
- If the system is not functional, learn why not
- Figuring out any changes or modifications
- Assessing the impact of these changes and modifications on the rest of the system

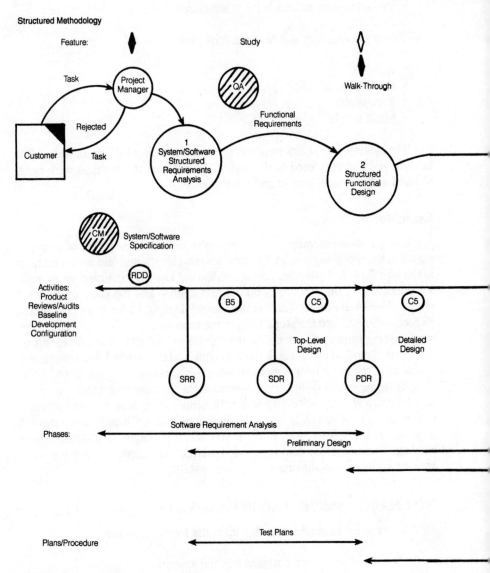

Figure 10.3. Computer system software methodology.

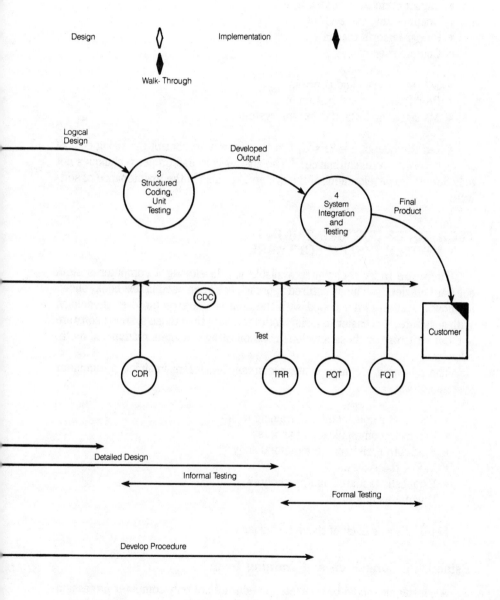

- Making changes and modifications
- Making the system workable
- Conduct thorough testings
- Impact on interfacing systems
- Documenting the system
- Prepare user's manuals
- Customer training
- Establish standards
- Set procedures and controls
- Productivity of the system
- Managing and Maintaining the system

Often the question is raised, "Is there a way to control the rising cost of computer software maintenance?" The answer is to use proper techniques not only during the development of the system, but also in the maintenance of software.

TECHNIQUES FOR MAINTAINING A COMPUTER SYSTEM SOFTWARE

There are many techniques available for developing a computer system software efficiently. The structured approach has been used in this book, showing how a system is developed with the help of the structured methodology. With structure, it is easier to maintain the software than those systems software without structure or those developed without proper documentation and methodology.

The following techniques are recommended for maintaining a computer system software:

- Establish a consultant and training team
- Eliminate communication barriers
- Eradicate resistance to a methodology
- Model the system
- Establish standards and procedures
- Update documentation

Let us discuss each of these techniques.

Establish a Consultant and Training Team

A consultant should be appointed to educate not only computer professionals, but also the customer. The roles of the consultant can be summarized as follows:

- To learn and educate others about the system to be maintained

- To conduct training for computer specialists, analysts, designers and programmers about state-of-the-art computer science technology
- To make the system more efficient and productive
- To show guidelines for improving maintenance techniques
- To instruct others on the use of effective maintenance tools
- To keep abreast of state-of-the-art knowledge
- To prepare plans for the future training
- To schedule classes, seminars or one-on-one technical training
- To show paths to success in maintaining a system cost effectively and in a timely way

Eliminate Communication Barriers

There is a communication barrier at all stages and phases of the computer software maintenance period. This barrier was discussed in Chapter 3, where a structured walk-through is explained as a good tool to eliminate a communication barrier. Another approach is to write less descriptive reports and show more logic in the graphics—there is less ambiguity in graphics. Most people can understand a picture better than hundreds of words of description.

There is a school of thought that says a fourth or fifth generation language of software development may take care of software maintenance. This is a great hope: that, one day, there will be a tool which may help develop and maintain an automatically cost-effective software. Until such a language is brought on-line, however, there will be a communication problem among the system developers, maintainers and the customers. We are lucky the tools of graphics and structured walk-throughs can solve the communication barrier to some extent when properly utilized.

Eradicate Resistance to a Methodology

It is human nature to resist any new things or changes in existing circumstances. It is no wonder that computer managers sometimes don't want to take chances when they are getting very little information from an existing inefficient system software; they are scared that a change might take away the information they are getting now and leave them with nothing. On the other hand, you have to take a chance in order to improve the maintenance environment of a system. Trying some of the tools used in modeling a system at this point may help improve maintenance.

Some might object to the idea of introducing a methodology at this level. Their idea may be that a methodology should be introduced at the development stages and not at the maintenance phase. They may insist that the system is productive to some extent and that it needs only maintenance. Let us take a practical approach and convince them to accept a methodological approach at maintenance level by showing the benefits of drawing a model of the system.

Model the System

A model of the system that is productive and easy to understand can be created easily. The model should take a graphic form so that it can be understood quickly. It does not have to be expensive.

Graphic models have been explained in detail in Chapters 3 and 4. Let's take an example to see the flexibility and benefits of modeling:

One of the duties of a system analyst is to estimate time in accordance with the requirements. This might affect some changes to be made in modules, units, and/or a component of a computer system's software and its files.

The system is in production, you are maintaining the system, and are accepting the benefits of the structured methodology. A sample model is shown in Figure 10.4.

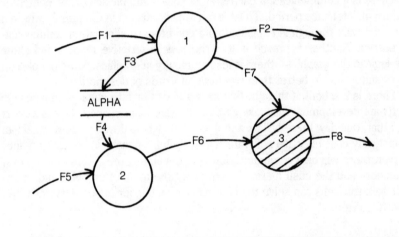

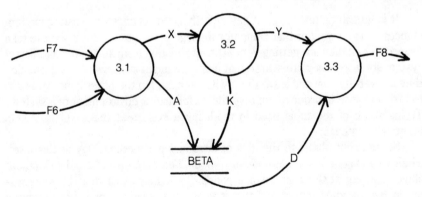

Figure 10.4. Sample model.

After analyzing the requirements, you conclude that the computer system designers and programmers need to make some changes in process 3.2 of the system model in the LDFD (Figure 10.4). Next, you must identify how many more files and processes will be affected in the LDFD figure.

Please spend some time and see if you can reach the decision of finding the correct answer. The solution is shown in the following pages.

The advantage of drawing a model of the system is that it can be done cost effectively and efficiently. You do not have to study a documented volume of books, complicated software listings or logical flow charts. Just refer to the unit level of the LDFD. In the model, the input to the process 3.2 may not be affected, but the output data flows K and Y will definitely be affected by the changes. The file "BETA" will be affected, and the process 3.3 will be affected, also.

Once you know the number of processes and files being affected with the changes, you can easily estimate the time and manpower needed to be utilized, presuming you already know the number of lines of code your module/unit consists of.

For example:

Refer to the same model and LDFD in Figure 10.4. As a computer analyst, you have received the requirements. After careful study of the requirements, you realize that there needs to be some changes made in the file "ALPHA".

You can immediately refer to the model and identify in no time where the file is located. You can also conclude that some other processes and files will be affected. Take some time now to identify how many more files and processes will be affected in the LDFD.

The file "ALPHA" is at level 1. Any changes occur at this level will affect many files, modules, and units at lower levels. The changes will affect the following:

- Process #2
- Process #1

Depending upon the logic of the system there might be some changes in the process #3. With changes in process #3, there also will be changes in level 2 of that process. The benefits of having a model is that it helps identify the changes affecting others files, modules, units and components.

Plan and Establish Standards and Procedures

Planning is very important in maintaining a system software. It is well-known that if you rush while developing a system, it takes almost double the time and cost to maintain that systems software.

The computer industry is a billion-dollar industry that needs proper planning, procedures and standards. The procedures should be consistently implemented and they must clearly define the rules and regulations to be adopted in the maintenance environment: what type of training is required to perform that particular task; what types of standards are enforced; and what is expected from workers. Rules and regulations are applied for quality assurance. The following guidelines for plans and rules are recommended:

- Keep them simple
- Make them effective
- Make them understandable
- Make them easy to follow
- Consider availability of tools
- Provide training to use those tools
- Create standards for maintenance
- Create procedures to follow
- Ensure quality of work
- Implement standards and procedures

Update Documentation

Continually update all the documentation. Any changes or patches should be registered in all the relevant documentation of the system model, and software listings should be updated and fully recorded. Don't hesitate to create new documentation if you have to do so to understand the system or draw a complete model of the system. You may think that this will take extra effort and manpower, but it is worth it. You will save a lot of manpower and time later on when you have a complete model of the system for quick reference when you are making changes in accordance with the requirements.

Often during the maintenance of a system, the question is asked, "Why create other documents like the LDFD or the logical structured system charts when we have the source listings of the system. Everything is included in the source listings." We do not deny the fact that source listings contain everything, but there are hundreds of lines of code in the system source listing. For a change to be made in accordance with the requirements, you have to go through all these codes to dig out the information. This is not only time-consuming and expensive, but frustrating.

Other questions asked are "Do we have logical flow charts to support the source listings? Why do we need any other document?" A conventional logical flow chart is shown in Figure 10.5. Logical flow charts are a great help in coding, but they don't show the following facts:

- Accessing of files
- Components called a unit/module

UNIT DETAILED DESIGN

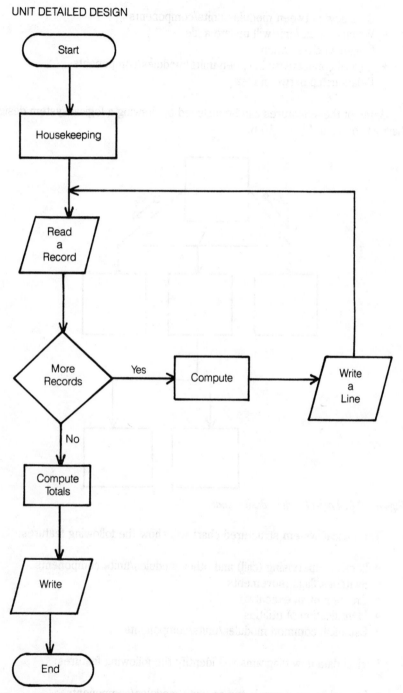

Figure 10.5. Conventional flowchart.

- Data flow between modules/units/components
- Which module/unit will update a file
- Flags/switches action
- Logical connectivity between units/modules/components
- Relationship between files

Some of these features can be included by drawing a logical system design chart as shown in Figure 10.6.

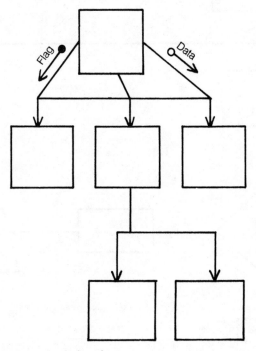

Figure 10.6. Logical system design chart.

The logical system structured chart will show the following features:

- Logical supervising (call) and other modules/units/components
- Switches/flags movements
- Creation of an executive
- Identification of utilities
- Establish common modules/units/components

Logical data flow diagrams will identify the following features:

- Logical connectivity between units/modules/components
- Data flows between files and units/modules/components

- Accessing of data files
- Updating data files
- Relationship among files

A logical data flow diagram of a system is shown in Figure 10.7.

This practically completes the modeling and documentation of a system. You can also include entity relationship diagrams and system states transition diagrams, or any other relevant diagram to better understand the system. The important thing is to keep these documents updated.

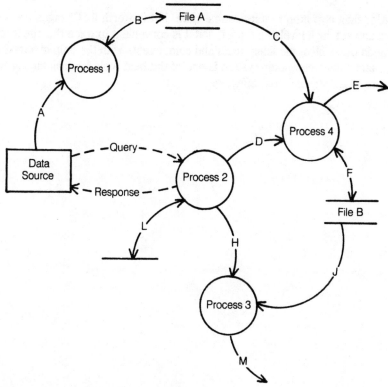

Figure 10.7. Logical data flow/diagram.

SUMMARY

The computer system software originates in the vendor's response to the request for proposal and the acceptance by the customer. The vendor establishes the system software development or maintenance team which receives a number of technical manuals, source and object listings and necessary documents concerning the system. The primary job of the team is to see that the system begins and continues in production.

The necessity of modeling the system is to meet the new requirements, to understand the system thoroughly and to satisfy the customer. You need to know:

- What logic governs the system functionality
- How modules/units/components are logically linked together
- How the files are logically accessed
- Which module/unit/component is updating a file
- How the logic will be affected by a change
- How to estimate and schedule correctly to implement a change

Modeling a system requires some time, but is worth it. Changes are seldom made at a high level of a model, and it is convenient to trace the effect of a change in other files, modules, units and components with the help of a model. Thus, modeling a computer system is one of the best tools for maintaining the software efficiently and cost effectively.

11

Systems Life-Cycle Software Maintenance

Software maintenance covers system life-cycle phases from the change requirement analysis to implementation. The maintenance may vary depending upon whether the change is minor or major. A minor change may require less effort and fewer changes in the software maintenance development phases, whereas, a major change is complex and may require great effort to change almost all the software maintenance development phases and documents. Sometimes, it is better to produce a software maintenance plan for a major change explaining the feasibility of achieving the change. It may be cost-effective to design a new system software if proper documentation and models of the system to be maintained are not available.

Ideally, the professionals who develop the system software should be the ones who maintain it. Those professionals are familiar with the system software and can maintain it most efficiently and cost effectively.

SOFTWARE REQUIREMENTS CHANGES

A new requirement for a change will be analyzed thoroughly by an analysis specialist to determine the effect upon the model of the system. He may have to form a team of experts if the workload is extensive.

The analyst is the one who will determine whether the change is feasible or not and will recommend if it is better to develop a new system or to make changes in the existing system software model. He will verify whether the change is minor or major and if it is cost effective. The analyst will also confirm the change requirements to be made in the system software engineering and estimate the time and schedule for completing the changes. Finally, he will draft a software maintenance plan and submit it to the management for approval.

The software maintenance plan (SMP) will include the following major fields:

- Labor
- Estimated cost
- Schedule
- Statement of work
- Documentation
- Milestones
- Facilities
- Environment
- Budget

Management will approve the plan to go ahead with the changes scheduled for implementation, as illustrated in Figure 11.1.

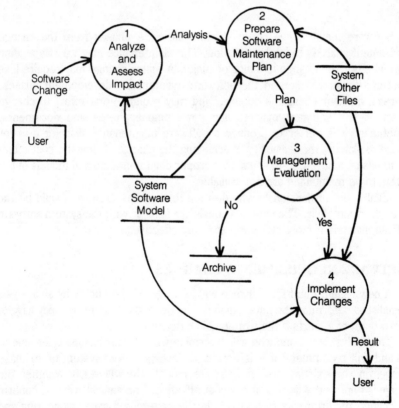

Figure 11.1. Software requirements change.

SYSTEM SOFTWARE MODELING

The system software model which was created during the software development is like a blueprint of the software engineering maintenance. It is appropriate to consider a software model as helpful not only for developing a system software, but also as a handy tool for maintaining the software. A change in the software engineering starts a chain reaction—it may affect many components, units and files. A model can give a clear and detailed picture of the affected parts of the system software engineering.

As explained earlier in this book, a software model will help to estimate easily the effect of the changes in various fields of the software engineering. It is a fact that to maintain a building or a bridge or a machine, the maintenance engineer needs its blueprints. Similarly, to maintain expensive system software engineering, a computer specialist needs its blueprints. The only difference is that, in the case of software engineering, the blueprint is the model of the system consisting of various software development phases and its products.

It is not easy to maintain a system without its model and proper documentation, and it is difficult to process maintenance if you don't understand the system software engineering. The model and other necessary documents will help a professional understand the system and the changes to be made in the system software engineering. If necessary, new documents are to be generated to complete the model. Proper training is sometimes necessary to understand the system software engineering methodology and the coding language.

Again, any changes which are made to the model should be updated to keep it effective for the future. A sample of the system software engineering model phases is shown in Figure 11.2.

SYSTEM SOFTWARE ANALYSIS

System software analysis for maintenance will proceed in the same manner as shown earlier for the software development phases, leading to the implementation and performance of all the necessary steps.

Analysis starts after the validity of the changes is established. This will establish the exact conditions under which the problem which necessitates the change occurs. It is better to gather additional information regarding the failure which caused the problem that is bringing about the change. Identify the conditions that caused the problem to happen. This may help identify similar circumstances so similar problems will not occur.

The findings of the analysis specialist will be reflected in the system software data flow diagrams, data dictionary and files. Appropriate changes should be made in those documentations for future reference. All other documentation that is a product of this phase should be changed, also. These documents will be reviewed and the incorporated changes will be approved by the user.

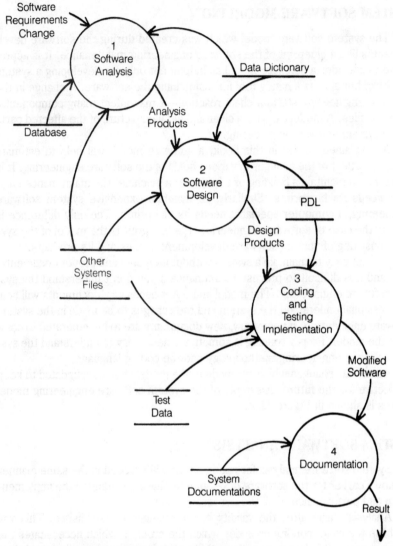

Figure 11.2. Software engineering phases (maintenance).

SYSTEM SOFTWARE DESIGN

The impact of the changes made in the structured analysis will be reflected in the system software design; this phase is the transformation of the functions of the change requirements identified in the previous phase.

The design consists of two phases:

- Top-level design
- Detailed design

The changes in the data flow diagrams will reflect the changes in the system logical design phase and may include some changes in components in the top-level, lower-level and units. The changes will also affect PDL and database files. The executive may be redesigned or modified depending upon the impact of the changes in the software engineering. All the documentation which is the product of this phase will be properly reviewed and updated. There will be changes in the program logical design phase. Logical flow charts may have to be restructured, and there may be some changes incorporated into the test plans and procedures.

Software Source and Object Code

Changes will affect the source code, and there may be need to code and debug some of the components/units. The procedure for testing will repeat now as it did during the software development phases.

Components integration testing will be conducted once the unit tests are satisfied, and all the verified units will be threaded together in a component and tested again. The techniques and standards will be followed in the same way as described for software development. A system integration test will be conducted following the techniques and procedures as explained previously. Test results should be acceptable to the user.

Update Software Documentation

All the documentation that is affected by the changes will be either updated or rewritten, along with the database files and data dictionary. Test documentation, system generation for productivity and actual changed source and object codes will be provided to the user. Any updated support documentations like quality evaluation, MANPRINT, test data and configuration management which are affected by the changes will also be delivered to the user.

SOFTWARE CHANGES SUMMARY

The software changes summary summarizes and records all the changes, minor or major, which are made in the system software. It gives the necessary information of how a problem occurred and under what circumstances. The document also keeps record of all the statistics about changes made in the system software. Some of the major activities affected and recorded are mentioned below:

- Analysis—DFD's, database files, data dictionary
- Design—structured charts
- Detailed design—PDL, pseudocode, flow charts
- Source code, object code
- Test data

- Job control procedures
- Integration test data
- Interface complexity
- System operation guidelines
- Critical checkpoints in maintaining the software
- Guidelines for the changes which should be made in the system software engineering
- Can avoid any potential problem
- Any word of caution in identifying a bug
- Routine checkups for productivity
- Any suggestions to keep the system software efficiently productive
- Safety precaution measures
- History of all the events
- Concluding strategy

SUMMARY

This chapter discussed techniques to maintain systems life-cycle software engineering. An analyst reviews and assesses a software change proposal and then creates a software maintenance plan which consists of a software change proposal preparation.

We also explained that to implement changes, one has to study and understand the existing software engineering model. This may involve creating additional models and other necessary documents if proper ones do not exist.

Modification of the software analysis, design, and source code in accordance with the required changes was explored. Proper testing to validate the changes in the software engineering and updating of all the necessary documents which are affected by the changes were explained.

Finally, we discussed how a software changes summary is created to register all the events and activities which took place in implementing these changes. This summary is a permanent record which includes many more entries detailing strengths and weaknesses of the system software engineering life-cycle maintenance.

Appendix

Acronyms and Abbreviations

APSE	Ada Programming Support Environment
ATD	Actual To Date
CDR	Critical Design Review
CDRL	Contract Data Requirements List
CM	Configuration Management
CSC	Computer Software Component
CSCI	Computer Software Configuration Item
CSD	Computer Systems Development
CSDM	Computer Software Development Methodology
CSDP	Computer Systems Development Plan
DBA	Database Administrator
DDA	Data Dictionary Administrator
DOD	Department of Defense
ERD	Entity Relationship Diagram
FCA	Functional Configuration Audit
FQR	Formal Qualification Review
HOL	High Order Language
HWCI	Hardware Configuration Item
IRS	Interface Requirements Specification
LDFD	Logical Data Flow Diagram
LLCSC	Lower Level Computer Software Component
MANPRINT	Manpower Integration
MPD	Main Process Diagram
PCA	Physical Configuration Audit
PDL	Program Design Language
PDR	Preliminary Design Review

PERT	Program Evaluation and Review Technique
PLD	Program Logical Design
QA	Quality Assurance
SDR	System Design Review
SEDP	Software Engineering Development Plan
SLD	System Logical Design
SMP	Software Maintenance Plan
SRLA	System Requirements Logical Analysis
SRR	System Requirements Review
SSR	Software Specification Review
SSTD	System States Transition Diagram
TLCSC	Top Level Computer Software Component
TRR	Test Readiness Review

Bibliography

"Balancing Project Management Software with Management Philosophies." *Federal Computer Week,* (September 28, 1987).

Budgen, David, and Richard Sincovec. "Introduction to Software Design." SEI Curriculum Module SEI-CM-2-1.2 (Preliminary), July 1987.

Chmura, J. Louis, and F. Henry Ledgard. *Cobol with Style.* Hasbrouck Heights, N.J.: Hayden Book Co., Inc., 1976.

Collofello, James S. "The Software Technical Review Process." SEI Curriculum Module SEI-CM-3-1.2 (Preliminary), July 1987.

————. "Introduction to Software Verification and Validation." SEI Curriculum Module SEI-CM-13-1.0, October 1987.

DeMarco, T. *Structured Analysis and System Specification.* Englewood Cliffs, N.J.: Prentice Hall, 1979.

Dickinson, Brian. *Developing Structured Systems.* New York: Yourdon Press, 1981.

Dijkstra, E. W., F. Dahl, and C. A. R. Hoare. *Structured Programming.* New York: Academic Press, 1972.

DOD Directive 5000.29, *Management of Computer Resources in Major Defense Systems.* 26 October 1976.

DOD Directive 5000.31, *Interim List of DOD Approved High Order Language (HOL).* 24 November 1976.

Firth, Robert, Vickey Mosley, Richard Pethia, Lauren Roberts, and William Wood. *A Guide to the Classification and Assessment of Software Engineering Tools.* Technical Report, Software Engineering Institute, Carnegie-Mellon University Pr., August 1987.

Firth, Robert, Bill Wood, Rich Pethia, Lauren Roberts, Vickey Mosley, and Tom Doice. *A Classification Scheme for Software Development Methods.* Technical Report, Software Engineering Institute, Carnegie-Mellon University Pr., November 1987.

Foreman, John, and John Goodenough. *Ada Adoption Handbook: A Program Manager's Guide.* Technical Report, Software Engineering Institute, Carnegie-Mellon University Pr., May 1987.

Formal Definition of the Ada Programming Language, (ii) France: Honeywell Inc., Honeywell-Bull and Inria, November 1980.

Freedman, Roy S. *Programming with APSE Software Tools.* Princeton, N.J.: Petrocelli Books, 1985.

Gane C., and T. Sarson. "Structured Systems Analysis: Tools and Techniques." Computer, July 1977.

Jackson, M. "The Jackson Design Methodology, Infotec State of the Art Report." *Structured Programming,* 1978.

Jorgensen, Paul C. "Requirements Specification Overview." SEI Curriculum Module SEI-CM-1-1.2 (Preliminary), July 1987.

Katzan, Harry. *Systems Design and Documentation.* New York: Van Nostrand Reinhold Co. Inc., 1976.

Kemerer, F. Chris. "An Empirical Validation of Software Cost Estimation Models." *Communication of the ACM,* vol. 30 no. 5, (May 1987), p. 416-429.

Kernighan W. Brian, and P. J. Plauger. *The Elements of Programming Style.* McGraw-Hill Bk. Co., 1974.

Leveson, Nancy G. "Software Safety." SEI Curriculum Module SEI-CM-6-1.1 (Preliminary), July 1987.

Lucas, Henry C. and Cyrus F. Gibson. *A Casebook for Management Information Systems.* McGraw-Hill Bk. Co., 1981.

Martin, James. *Computer Data-Base Organization.* Englewood Cliffs, N.J.: Prentice Hall, 1977.

Mills, Everald, E. "Software Metrics." SEI Curriculum Module SEI-CM-12-1.0, October 1987.

Morell, Larry J. "Unit Testing and Analysis." SEI Curriculum Module SEI-CM-9-1.0, October 1987.

Noll, Paul. *Structured Programming for the Cobol Programmers.* Mike Murach & Associates, Inc., 1977.

_____. *The Structured Programming Cook Book.* Fresno, Calif.: Mike Murach & Associates, Inc., 1978.

Scacchi, Walt. "Models of Software Evolution: Life Cycle and Process." SEI Curriculum Module SEI-CM-10-1.0, October 1987.

Shelly B. Gary, and J. Thomas Cashman. *Advanced Structured Cobol.* Belmont, Calif.: Anaheim Publishing Company, 1978.

Sodhi, Jag. "Efficient Techniques for Analysis, Design, and Programming." *Scientific and Business Systems,* unpublished 1982.

_____. "A Methodology for Software Engineering Development Life Cycle." Seminar, 1986.

_____. *A Handbook for Structured Walkthroughs.* 1986.

_____. *Structured Analysis for Real-time Systems, Student's Handbook.* 1987.

_____. *Software Engineering Requirements Analysis (SERA), Student's Handbook.* 1988.

_____. *Software Engineering Design, (SED), Student's Handbook.* 1988.

_____. *Managing Ada Projects Using Software Engineering.* Blue Ridge Summit, Penn.: TAB BOOKS Inc., 1990.

Tufts, Lt. Col. J. Robert, USAF. "Advanced DBMS Concepts." Association for Computing Machinery.

U.S. Dept. of Defense, Military Standard, *Defense System Software Development.* DOD-STD-2167, Washington, D.C.

_____. Military Standard, *Defense System Software Development.* DOD-STD-2167A, Washington, D.C.

_____. Military Standard, *Software Quality Evaluation.* DOD-STD-2168 (DRAFT), 26 April 1985.

_____. Joint Regulation, *Management of Computer Resources in Defense Systems.* 7 May 1985.

_____. *Reference Manual for the Ada Programming Language.* ANS/MIL-STD-1815A, Jan 1983.

Ward, T. Paul, and Stephen J. Mellor. *Structured Development for Real-Time Systems.* Vol. I, II, III, Yourdon Press, Englewood Cliffs, N.J.: Prentice Hall, 1985.

Warnier, J. D. and Kenneth T. Orr. *Structured Systems Development.* New York: Yourdon Press, 1977.

Weinberg, G. M. *The Psychology of Computer Programming.* New York: Von Nostrand Reinhold, 1971.

Welderman, Nelson H. "Criteria for Constructing and Using an Ada Embedded System Testbed." Technical Report, SEI, Carnegie-Mellon University, November 1987.

Wetherbe, James C. *Systems Analysis and Design.* St. Paul, Minn.: West Publishing Company, 1984.

Yourdon, Edward Nash. *Classics in Software Engineering.* New York: Yourdon Press, 1979.

_____. *Structured Walkthroughs.* New York: Yourdon Press, 1978.

Yourdon, Edward, and L. Larry Constantine. *Structured Design.* New York: Yourdon Press, 1978.

Index

A

abbreviations and acronyms, 153-154
acronyms and abbreviations, 153-154
Ada, ix, 43, 113
atmosphere, working, 27

B

bar charts, 92
batch systems, 3
bidder's responsibilities, 10-13
  checklist for, 12-13
  pricing, 11
  RFP, 9
budgeting, 20

C

charts, 92-93
  flow charts, 111-113, 144
  Nassi-Shneiderman (NS), 114, 116
Chen entity relationship diagram, 83
COBOL, 114, 123
coding, 35, 52
  conventions and standards, 118
  language selection, 121
  pseudo code, 114, 116
  source and object code, 151
communications, 30, 48
  barrier elimination, 139
  effectiveness of, 27
computer-aided software engineering
  (CASE), 46

computer software component (CSC), 98
  testing, 122, 124
computer software configuration item
  (CSCI), 98
  system breakdown and organization, 105
computer software development methodology (CSDM), 33
  selection of, 43, 46, 43
  structured techniques for, 46
computer systems project (*see* projects)
concept exploration phase, 35
configuration item, 98
  testing, 35
Constantine, 46
consultant team, software maintenance
  techniques, 138
context diagram, SRLA, 59-60
contract data requirements list (CDRL), 35
controls, top-level system structured
  design, 101
cost estimation algorithm, 9-10
critical path, 22
customer acceptance of system, 127

D

data
  classes of, 78
  databases for, 81
  dictionary for (*see* data dictionary)
  elements of, 79
  entity relationship diagramming for, 81-83
  file structures for, 80-81

flow diagram, 66
  groups of, 79
  management of (*see* data management)
  structuring, 118
data dictionary, 67, 77-80, 104, 118
  data classes in, 78
  data elements, 79
  data group, 79
  element definition in, 78
  requirements of, 78
data management, 77-85
  data dictionary for, 77
  databases, 81
  entity relationship diagram (ERD) for, 81-83
  file structure, 80-81
  overview of processes in, 84
data structured design, 102
databases, 81, 104
decision tables, 90
decision trees, 91
decision-assisting devices, 89-93
  charts, 92-93
  decision tables, 90
  decision trees, 91
  graphics, 91
delegation of responsibilities, 20
deliverables, RFP, 9
Demarco, 46
demonstration and validation phase, 35
Department of Defense (DOD), 34
design (*see also* detailed design phase; preliminary design phase)
  data structured, 102
  logical, system (SLD), 97-105
  object-oriented, 101-102
  program (*see* program logical design)
  system software, 150
destinations, data, 66
detailed design phase, 35, 52
development and implementation techniques, 107-129
development cycle, software, 40-41
Dijkastra, E.W., viii, 46
direct organization, 18
documentation, 126
  RFP, 8
  updating, 142, 151
DOD-STD-2167, viii, 34-43
DOD-STD-2167A, 35, 42, 43

E

earned value estimation technique, 21

embedded applications, 43
engineering techniques, 31-105
English, structured (*see* structured English)
entity relationship diagram (ERD), 81-83
  Chen, 83
  Merise, 83
environment, RFP, 8
estimating and scheduling, 21-24
  critical path, 22
  earned value technique, 21
  Gantt technique, 23
  PERT technique, 22
evaluation phase, 127-128
event list, 61-63
expert systems, 3

F

feasibility study, 4-5
file structures, 80-81, 104
  temporary vs. permanent files, 80
flowchart, 111-113, 144
  data, 65, 66
  system, 61
full-scale development, 35
functional organization, 18
functions, RFP, 8

G

Gane, 46
Gantt technique, 23-24
goal setting, 20
graphics, decision-making, 91

H

hierarchical levels, top-level system structured design, 98
high order languages (HOL), 43, 118
HIPO, 114, 115

I

IF-THEN-ELSE statements, 117
  nested, 117
implementation, 121-129
  coding langauges, 121
  computer software component (CSC) testing, 122, 124
  customer acceptance, 127
  documentation, 126
  evaluation, 127-128
  productivity testing, 126
  system integration testing, 124-125
  unit/module testing, 122

input/output formats, 119
integration and testing phase, 35

J

Jackson, 46

K

knowledge-based systems, 3

L

languages
  COBOL, 123
  high-order (HOL), 43, 118
  program design (PDL), 113
  selection of, 121
leveling, LDFD, 67-70
life cycle software maintenance, 131-152
life cycle, system, 35, 52
  concept exploration phase, 35
  demonstration and validation phase, 35
  development cycle within, 36-37
  full-scale development phase, 35
  production and deployment phase, 35
  software maintenance and, 147-152
  support cycle within, 38-39
line charts, 92
logic blocks, 87-89
logical data flow diagram (LDFD), 63-66,
  104, 141, 145
  data destination in, 66
  data flow in, 65
  data process in, 65
  data source in, 65
  data store in, 65
  drawing tips, 64
  error checking in, 65
  example of, 71-75
  naming conventions, 67
  partitioning, 67-70
  properties of, 71-75
  proposed standards, 70
logical flowchart, 111-113
logical specifications, 87-95, 104
  decision-assisting devices, 89-93
  structured English for, 87
  system states transition diagram (SSTD),
  93-95

M

main process diagram (MPD), 59-60
management techniques, 24-28
  communication effectiveness, 27

control, 25, 27, 25
data (see data management)
manpower integration (MANPRINT), 28
milestone development, 25, 26
standards establishments, 27
technical training program development,
  27
workable atmosphere creation, 27
manpower integration (MANPRINT), 28
matrix organization, 18
menu-driven systems, 3
Merise entity relationship diagram, 83, 84
mesh-DFD, 62
methodologies, 33
  eradicating resistance to, 139
  software, 136
MIL-STD-1815A, 43
milestones, 25, 26
mini specifications, 67, 87-88
modeling, 51, 53-57
  child structure, 143
  goals of, 55
  parent structure, 140
  structure and function of, 55
  system software, 149
module testing, 122

N

Nassi-Shneiderman (NS) charts, 114, 116
nested IF-THEN-ELSE statements, 117,
  118
NS charts, 114, 116

O

object code, 151
object-oriented design, 101-102
objectives statement, RFP, 7
on-line systems, 3
organizational planning, 18-19
Orr, 46

P

parent/child structure, 68, 140, 143
partitioning, 67-70
  balancing of, 67
  leveling, 67-70
  naming LDFD, 67
  numbering techniques, 67
  parent/child structures, 68
permanent files, 80, 81
personnel (see staffing and)
PERT technique, 22

Index

pie charts, 92
preliminary design phase, 35, 52
preliminary study of systems, 4
pricing guidelines, 11
procedures, establishment of, 141
processes, data, 65
production and deployment phase, 35
productivity, 126
program design language (PDL), 113
program logical design, 109-120
  coding conventions and standards, 118
  HIPO, 114, 115
  IF-THEN-ELSE statements, 117
  input/output formats, 119
  logical flow chart, 111-113
  Nassi-Shneiderman (NS) charts, 114, 116
  nested IF-THEN-ELSE statements, 117, 118
  products of, 119
  program design language (PDL), 113
  pseudo code, 114, 116
  report formats, 119
  testing, 119
  top-down concept, 109-111
programs
  COBOL example, 123
  logical design of, 109-120
  top-level system structured design. 98-101
project manager, 17
  delegation of responsibilities for, 20
  functions of, 24-25
projects, 17-30
  budget planning for, 20
  delegation of functional responsibilities, 20
  estimating and scheduling, 21-24
  goal setting, 20
  management techniques for, 24-28
  organizational planning for, 18-19
  planning steps for, 19-21
  project manager for, 17
  staffing, 20
  system manager for, 17
pseudo code, 114, 116
pure project organization, 18

R

real-time systems, 3
records, 81
report formats, 119
request for proposal (RFP), 5-9
  bidder's responsibilities, 9, 10
  evaluation of, 9
  flow of procedures for, 15
  format of, 9
  main features of, 6-9
  outline for, 6
requirements analysis, 5
  logical (*see* system requirements logical analysis)
  RFP, 8
  software, 35, 52
responsibilities, delegation of, 20
reviews, 104

S

Sarson, 46
scheduling, 21-24
scope statement, RFP, 8
software
  methodologies for, 136
  source and object code, 151
  structured computer system, 133
  system, analysis of, 149
  system, design, 150
  system, modeling, 149
  types of, 133-135
  unstructured computer system, 133
software components (*see* computer software components (CSC)
software engineering, 33-57
  acceptance procedures, 103
  Ada impact on, 43
  CDSM selection, 43
  coding and unit testing phase, 35, 52
  computer aided (CASE), 46
  computer software component (CSC) integration and testing p, 35
  computer software configuration item (CSCI) testing, 35
  computer software development methodology (CSDM), 33
  detailed design phase, 35, 52
  development activities flowchart, 44-45
  development cycle within system life cycle, 36-37
  DOD-STD-2167 in, 34
  life cycle, system, 35, 52
  modeling systems, 53-57
  phases of, 35, 150
  phases of, duration, 54
  preliminary design phase, 35, 52
  software development cycle, 40-41
  software maintenance, 133-146

software requirements analysis, 35, 52
  structured techniques for, 46-51
  testing procedures, 103
software maintenance, 133-146
  communications barriers elimination, 139
  consultant and training teams, 138
  cost of, 135
  cost trends, systems, 134
  documentation updating, 142, 151
  eradicating resistance to methodology, 139
  flowcharting, 144
  logical data flow diagram (LDFD), 145
  modeling systems, 140
  software requirements changes, 147
  software types, 133-135
  source and object code, 151
  standards and procedures establishment, 141
  structured vs. unstructured computer system software, 133
  summarizing changes, 151
  system life cycle and, 147-152
  system software analysis, 149
  system software design, 150
  system software modeling, 149
software maintenance plans (SMP), 148
source code, 151
sources, data, 65
specifications, 104
  logical (see logical specifications)
  mini-, 67, 87-88
staffing and personnel, 20
  manpower integration (MANPRINT), 28
  training programs for, 27
standards, 27
  coding, 118
  DOD-STD-2167A, 42
  establishment of, 141
  logical data flow diagram (LDFD), proposed, 70
statement of work (SOW), 10, 35
storage, data, 65
structured computer system software, 133
structured English, 87-89114
  mini specifications logic blocks, 87
structured methodologies, 46-51
  advantages of, 48
  communications and, 48
  diagram of, 47
  modeling a system, walk-through form, 51
  walk-through, structured, 48-51

structured walk-through, 48-51, 104
support cycle, system life cycle and, 38-39
switches, top-level system structured design, 101
system integration testing, 124-125
system logical design (SLD), 97-105
  acceptance procedure development, 103
  data structured design, 102
  object-oriented design, 101-102
  products of, 103-104
  structure diagram, 104
  system breakdown and CSCI organization, 105
  test procedure development, 103
  top-level structured, 98-101
system manager, 17
system requirements logical analysis (SRLA), 59-76
  context diagram, 59-60
  event list, 61-63
  LDFD example, 71-75
  listing requirements, 61-63
  logical data flow diagram, 63
  partitioning, 67-70
system states transition diagrams (SSTD), 93-95
systems, 3-16
  algorithm to estimate time and cost, 9-10
  cost trends, 134
  feasibility study of, 4-5
  preliminary study of, 4
  request for proposal for, 5
  requirements analysis for, 5

T

tables, decision, 90
temporary files, 80, 81
testing, 35, 52, 104
  computer software component (CSC), 35, 122, 124
  configuration items, 35
  procedure development for, 103
  productivity, 126
  system integration, 124-125
  unit/module, 122
time, estimation algorithm, 9-10
top-down concept, programming, 109-111
top-level system structured design, 98-101
  charting, 99
  controls/switches in, 101
  distinct computer programs for, 98-101
  efficient techniques for, 101
  hierarchical levels in, 98

training, 43
  developing programs for, 27
  maintenance techniques, software, 138
transition diagram, system state, 93-95
trees, decision, 91

U

unit testing phase, 35, 52, 122
unstructured computer system software, 133

V

visual table of contents (VTOC), 109-110

W

walk-through, structured, 48-51, 104
Warnier, 46

Y

Yourdon, 46